W0307321

Vorwort

Autonomie im Unterricht

Die vorliegenden Materialien zur Freiarbeit bieten den Schülern vielfältiges Material zur spielerischen Überprüfung gelernter Inhalte an. Dies ist für die Schüler gerade im Hinblick auf die weithin geforderte Lernerautonomie von großer Bedeutung.
Freiarbeit bedeutet vor allem selbstbestimmtes Arbeiten. Die Schüler werden dabei schrittweise dazu befähigt, Verantwortung für das eigene Lernen zu übernehmen. Sie haben hier die Möglichkeit, das eigene Lerntempo zu bestimmen.
Alle Materialien können von den Schülern anhand des Lösungsschlüssels am Ende des Heftes selbst überprüft werden, sodass der Lehrkraft an dieser Stelle des Unterrichts mehr die Rolle des Lernberaters zukommt. Die Lehrkraft kann sich dadurch vor allem den schwächeren Schülern zuwenden und unterstützend tätig werden. Auch sollte die Lehrkraft darauf achten, dass sich die Schüler bei Partner- und Gruppenarbeit in der Zielsprache austauschen und die angegebenen Redewendungen benutzen.

Spielerischer Lernprozess

Die vorliegenden Freiarbeitsmaterialien bieten oft spielerische Ansätze und sollen die Schüler dazu motivieren, sich mit der Zielsprache zu beschäftigen. Die Sammlung enthält neben Spielen auch Partnerarbeitsmaterialien, um das gemeinsame Lernen zu fördern. Wenn die Klassensituation dies ergibt, können bei Partnerübungen z.B. ein schwächerer und ein stärkerer Schüler zusammenarbeiten, wobei der stärkere dem schwächeren Schüler Hilfestellung bietet und dadurch auch sein eigenes Wissen festigt.

Binnendifferenzierung

Gerade in Klassen mit einem breiten Leistungsspektrum bieten sich die Freiarbeitsmaterialien auch für den Einsatz bei der Binnendifferenzierung an. So werden schwächere Schüler individuell gefördert und stärkere Schüler gefordert.

Zielgruppe

Die Freiarbeitsmaterialien sind für alle Ausgaben von English G 21, Band 2, konzipiert und unitweise aufgebaut. Die Materialien können sowohl einzeln als auch in Partnerarbeit bearbeitet werden. Langfristig wird so die soziale Kompetenz gefördert. Es ist von entscheidender Bedeutung, dass sich die Schüler gegenseitig helfen und korrigieren.

Benutzung der Materialien

In den Übersichtsseiten vor den Units wird der jeweilige Schwerpunkt der einzelnen Arbeitsblätter kenntlich gemacht. Dieser kann auf Grammatik, Redemitteln oder Wortschatz liegen. Dadurch können die Materialien sowohl im normalen Unterricht zur Vertiefung eines Schwerpunkts oder zur Wiederholung eingesetzt werden, ebenso wie in ausgewiesenen Freiarbeitsstunden.
Dort, wo etwas ausgeschnitten werden muss, wurde dies durch das Symbol der Schere kenntlich gemacht. Es bietet sich an, die Materialien zu folieren, um sie haltbar zu machen.

Inhalt

Unit-Überblick

Kopiervorlagen

	Nummer	Titel	Schwerpunkt
	3.2	When this lesson ends	Grammatikübung zum *will-future.*
	3.3	What will you do if …?	Grammatikübung zur Bildung von Konditionalsätzen Typ 1.
	3.4	Our crazy teacher	Grammatikübung zur Unterscheidung von Adjektiv und Adverb.
	3.5	TV – television	Wortschatzübung zum Thema *television.*
	3.6	Do you know what these animals need?	Schreibaufgabe zum Thema *animals.*
Unit 4	4.1	Parts of the body	Wortschatzübung zu den Themen *body parts, clothes, illnesses, injuries.*
	4.2	Word grid: Have you ever done this?	Grammatikübung zum Gebrauch der *past participles.*
	4.3	Word order	Grammatikübung zur Wiederholung der Satzstruktur im Englischen.
	4.4	An e-mail from Wales	Übung zum Leseverstehen mit anschlie-ßendem Schreibauftrag.
	4.5	Can or may?	Grammatikübung zu *can* und *may.*
	4.6	What happened?	Grammatikübung zur Wiederholung des *simple past* im Bericht.
Unit 5	5.1	Town and country	Wortschatzübung zum thema *town and country.*
	5.2	Shopping in the city	Grammatikübung zur Festigung der *question tags* im Dialog.
	5.3	Mind map: Your town	Schreibaufgabe zum Thema ‚*Your town*' mit vorbereitender *mind map.*
	5.4	Irregular verbs	Grammatikübung zur Wiederholung und Festigung der unregelmäßigen Verben.
	5.5	A very hard week in the life of Jenny Brown	Grammatikübung zur kontextgebundenen Anwendung der bekannten Zeiten.
	5.6	Can you find the way to the rocket?	Grammatikübung zur Wiederholung von *will-future* und *going to-future.*
Unit 6	6.1	Can you tell me the way please?	Übung zu Techniken der Wegbeschreibung an-hand eines Stadtplans.
	6.2	What's happening outside?	Grammatikübung zur Wiederholung und Festigung des *present progressive.*
	6.3	What were the students doing?	Grammatikübung zur Wiederholung und Festigung des *past progressive.*
	6.4	Who, which or that?	Grammatikübung zu den Relativpronomen.
	6.5	Let's play a game!	Festigung der Relativpronomen in spiele-rischer Form.
	6.6	A night at school	Grammatikübung zur Festigung der Verwendung von *mustn't* und *needn't.*

0.1 KV Focus on words: Holidays

a) *What do you think of when you think about holidays? Add words to the network.*

Was fällt dir ein, wenn du an Urlaub denkst? Füge dem network *Wörter hinzu.*

b) *Swap networks with a partner. Add more words to your partner's network.*

Tausche dein network *mit dem eines Partners und füge ihm mehr Wörter hinzu.*

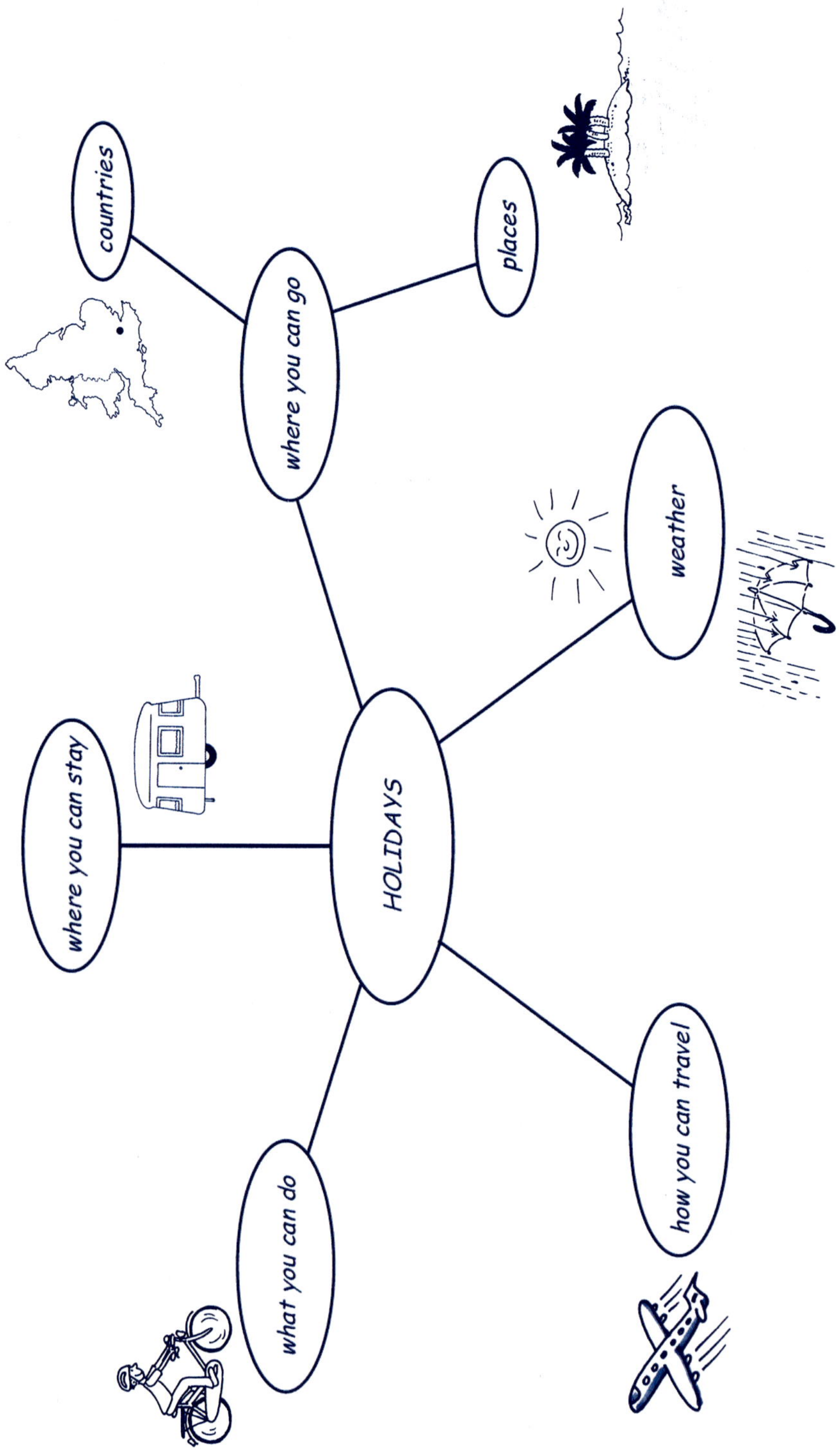

c) *Scrambled words: All the words have something to do with holidays.*
Write down the correct words.

Alle Wörter haben etwas mit dem Thema Urlaub zu tun. Schreib die richtigen Wörter auf.

You can go to …

Places

1 lkae ______________________

2 eas ______________________

3 hcbae ______________________

4 aintsnumo ______________________

Countries

5 rotacia ______________________

6 narfc ______________________

7 niaps ______________________

8 lytia ______________________

You can go by …

9 arc ______________________

10 nepal ______________________

11 nirat ______________________

12 ubs ______________________

You can stay in a …

13 helto ______________________

14 varcana ______________________

15 nett ______________________

16 laydhio talf ______________________

Activities: You can …

17 wims ______________________

18 ekat thoops ______________________

19 veah nuf ______________________

20 dire a kebi ______________________

The weather can be …

21 nynus ______________________

22 rawm ______________________

23 rynia ______________________

24 lodycu ______________________

Unit 1 – Überblick

KV 1.1 Connecting the numbers

Diese Wortschatzübung dient der Festigung des Wortschatzes aus Unit 1 auf spielerische Art und Weise. Es besteht die Möglichkeit der Selbstkontrolle durch das zu zeichnende Bild.

KV 1.2 Describing pictures

Schwerpunkt dieser Übung ist das Beschreiben eines Bildes in Form eines Fließtextes. Die S bearbeiten Lückentexte mit steigendem Schwierigkeitsgrad, bis sie zuletzt in der Lage sind, einen kurzen Text selbstständig zu verfassen.

KV 1.3 Role cards: Asking questions

Partnerarbeit: Hier wird das Formulieren von Fragen in der Zielsprache anhand von Hilfeboxen geübt. Mithilfe der Fragen vervollständigen die S ihre lückenhaften *role cards*. Nach drei Karten wird getauscht.

KV 1.4 Reading and writing: Tom's holidays in Croatia

Der Schwerpunkt dieser KV liegt auf dem Leseverstehen und dem Schreiben mit offenem Schreibauftrag. Mit einer leichteren Einstiegsaufgabe zum Textverständnis werden die S auf das Verfassen eines eigenen Textes vorbereitet.

KV 1.5 Telling a story: Tom's first day at school

Hier wird eine Geschichte ausgehend von einem Bilderpuzzle erzählt. Die S bringen die Bilder zunächst in die richtige Reihenfolge. Dann schreiben sie die Geschichte unter Verwendung von *linking words* und *time phrases* auf.

KV 1.6 Information gap: The last party

Partnerarbeit: Schwerpunkt dieser Übung ist die Verwendung des *simple past* in Fragen und Antworten. In der Tabelle von Partner A befinden sich Antworten und Informationslücken. Diese sind in der Tabelle von Partner B gefüllt, sodass beide Tabellen im Frage-Antwort-Spiel vervollständigt werden können.

*Find the hidden picture! Complete **a)** and **b)** to find out what it is.*

***a)** Fill in the gaps.*

Ergänze die fett gedruckten Wörter im englischen Satz.

1	**Beschreibe** das Foto bitte!	_ _ _ _ [_] _ _ _ the photo, please.
2	Das ist mir zu **gefährlich**.	This is too _ _ _ _ _ _ _ [_] _ for me.
3	Das ist **erstaunlich**.	That's _ _ _ [_] _ _ _.
4	Es gibt viele berühmte **Sehenswürdigkeiten** in London.	There are many famous _ _ _ _ [_] _ in London.
5	Im Moment klappt **nichts**.	_ _ _ _ _ _ [_] is going right at the moment.
6	Das ist eine gute **Erklärung**.	That's a good _ _ [_] _ _ _ _ _ _ _ _.
7	Wir hatten **aufregende** Ferien.	We had _ [_] _ _ _ _ _ _ holidays.
8	Mir geht's schlecht. Ich hatte einen **Streit** mit meiner kleinen Schwester.	I feel bad. I had an [_] _ _ _ _ _ _ _ with my little sister.
9	Unser neuer Kunstlehrer ist **unfreundlich**.	Our new Arts teacher is _ _ _ [_] _ _ _ _ _ _.
10	Ich muss mich **zwischen** Tennis oder Hockey entscheiden.	I have to decide _ _ _ _ _ _ [_] tennis or hockey.
11	Unser **Flug** nach Spanien war schrecklich.	Our [_] _ _ _ _ _ to Spain was terrible.
12	Jakob rennt sehr **schnell**.	Jacob runs very _ _ [_] _.
13	**Nach** der Schule gehen wir noch in der Stadt einkaufen.	_ _ _ [_] _ school we go shopping in the city.
14	Es ist **unverschämt**, über andere Schüler zu lachen.	It's _ _ [_] _ to laugh about other pupils.
15	Kannst du mir den neuen *Harry Potter* **ausleihen**?	Can you [_] _ _ _ me the new *Harry Potter*?
16	Hannes ist **wütend** auf seinen Deutschlehrer.	Hannes is _ _ _ _ [_] with his German teacher.
17	Im **Vordergrund** kannst du meine Mutter und mich sehen.	In the _ _ [_] _ _ _ _ _ _ _ you can see my mother and I.

KV Connecting the numbers

b) *Here's the code to your hidden picture. The letters in the grey fields in **a)** stand for a number. Connect the numbers in the order of the questions.*

*Hier steht der Schlüssel zum verborgenen Bild. Die grau markierten Buchstaben aus **a)** stehen jeweils für eine Zahl. Verbinde die Zahlen in der Reihenfolge der Fragen.*

A = 49	E = 51	I = 11	M = 28	Q = 40	U = 33	Y = 12
B = 38	F = 39	J = 5	N = 37	R = 2	V = 8	Z = 6
C = 42	G = 3	K = 22	O = 29	S = 25	W = 7	
D = 31	H = 14	L = 43	P = 35	T = 47	X = 4	

c) *Now connect the numbers!*
What's the hidden picture?

38	30	7	18	24	48	56
44	15	40	51	21	34	53
17	50	31	25	5	23	16
55	43	8	39	45	10	22
19	42	12	37	29	36	41
26	6	33	2	49	4	32
27	1	14	46	20	13	28
9	52	47	3	35	11	54

Picture 1

Picture 2

Picture 3

KV Describing pictures

a) *Enter the missing words to describe picture 1:*

In this picture you can see our ____________. It's the one on the right. My father's ______________ is in front of our house. On the ___________ there is another house, it's the Smith's house. Toby Smith and I like to play ____________________ in the afternoon. There is a field right next to our house. Many big _____________ grow along our street. There's also a ____________________ next to Toby's house. You can buy nearly everything there. My little sister and her friends are playing outside at the moment. They like to ride their _________________ and play games.

b) *Enter the missing words and phrases to describe picture 2:*

In this picture ____. It's time for ____________________________! There are four people in my family, so there are four _______________________ and four ______________________. In the middle of the table, there are two ____ and tea. There is also some __________________________ on a plate, some ___________________________ and ____________________. Next to the bread is a big _________________. There are two _____________________, four _________________, and some _______________________ in the bowl.

c) *Now you! Write a text to describe picture 3:*

____

____

____

____

____

____

Remember:

Describing pictures

at the top/bottom • in the foreground/background • in the middle • on the left/right
behind • between • in front of • next to • under

a) *Cut out the role cards. Partner A gets the left part, Partner B the right part of each role card. Partner B asks Partner A questions and fills in the gaps. Look at **b)** if you need help. Then swap cards and check.*

*Schneidet die Rollenkarten aus. Partner A bekommt den linken, Partner B den rechten Teil jeder Rollenkarte. Partner B stellt Partner A Fragen. Schaut bei **b)** nach, wenn ihr Hilfe braucht. Danach könnt ihr tauschen und eure Ergebnisse überprüfen.*

Paul: watches TV every day listens to music for hours plays football every Thursday was on holiday in Spain	**Paul:** watches ____________ every day listens to music ____________ plays football ____________ was ____________ in Spain
Anna: was on holiday in Turkey speaks a little Turkish now liked the beach very much flew for the first time this year	**Anna:** was on holiday ____________ speaks ____________ now ____________ the beach very much flew for the ____________ time this year
Linda: is good at Maths visits her grandmother likes to read books plays piano	**Linda:** is good at ____________ visits ____________ ____________ to read books plays ____________
Gemma: is new in ____________ is ____________ to the others didn't want to ____________ sits ____________ in the classroom	**Gemma:** is new in Bristol is not very friendly to the others didn't want to come here sits near the window in the classroom
John: waits for ____________ doesn't like ____________ goes to bed at ____________ ____________ to school	**John:** waits for the teacher doesn't like school goes to bed at 9 o'clock rides his bike to school
Marc: has got ____________ does sports ____________ likes ____________ best often plays ____________	**Marc:** has got a brother does sports every day likes chocolate best often plays on his computer

b) *Asking questions:*

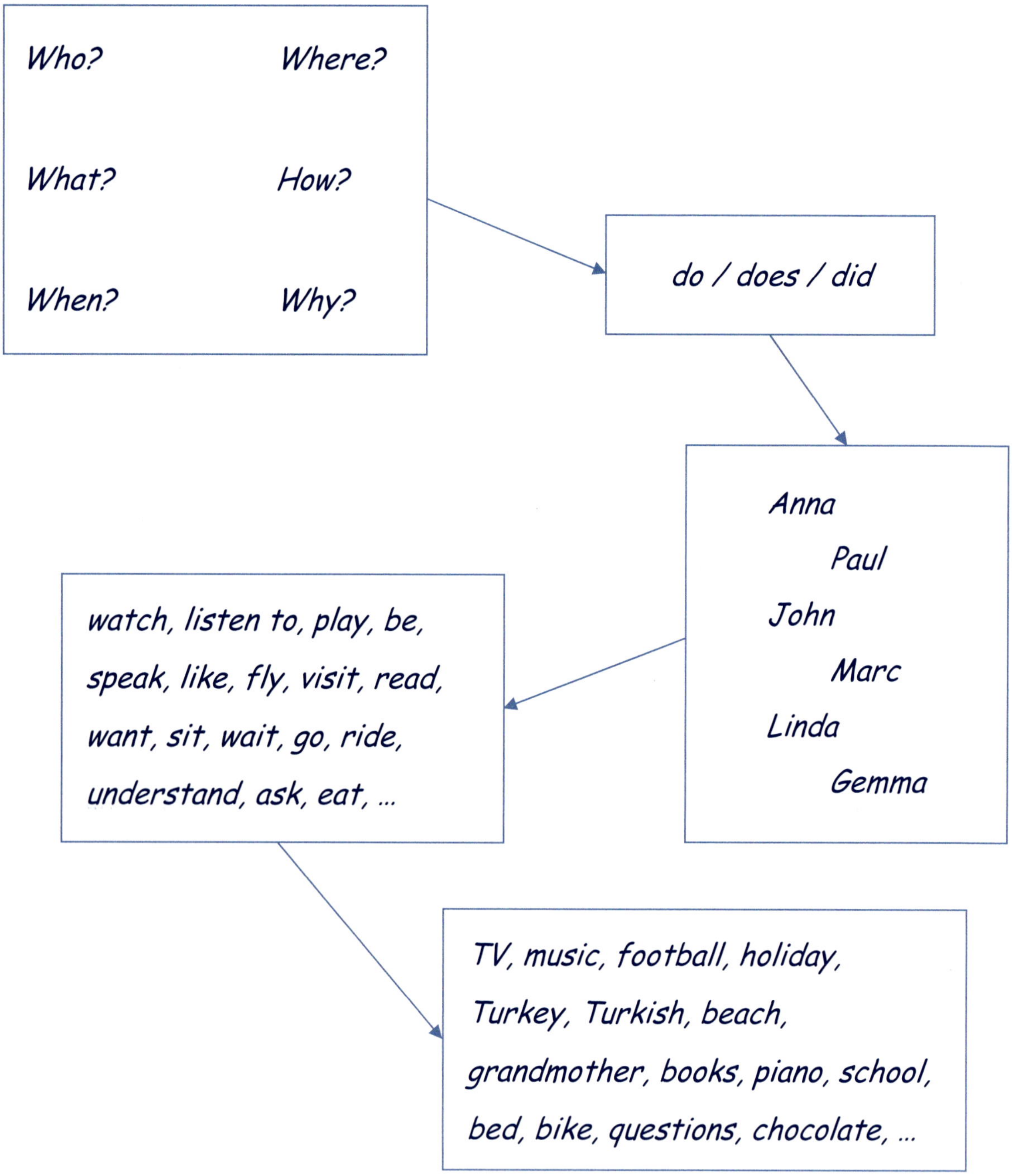

Remember:

Fragen bildet man im Englischen so:

Fragewort	+	do/does/did	+	Subjekt	+	Verb	+	Objekt
When	+	*did*	+	*Tom*	+	*call*	+	*his sister?*

a) Read about Tom's holidays.

Last summer, Tom Köhler went to Croatia with his family. They took the plane and flew to Zagreb airport. In Zagreb they hired a car[1] and went to Krk, a beautiful island with old cities and mountains. The weather was fantastic. It was sunny and sometimes very windy. They stayed at a campsite by the sea.
It was great! Every day Tom went swimming and played volleyball on the beach with a lot of other kids from Austria, Italy, Spain and Germany. They spoke English all the time and Tom learned a lot.
He went walking with his father too. From the top of the mountain they had a great view[2] of the countryside: green forests, brown hills and the blue sea.
One day they went to another island by boat. That was super too, because the waves were really big. It was fun for Tom! But his sister didn't like the trip. She was sick on the boat. Poor Emily!
When the holidays were over after two weeks, they were all very sad. They said goodbye to everybody, but Tom still[3] writes e-mails to Maria, a girl from Spain …

b) Right or wrong? Tick (✓) the correct box. Correct the wrong statements.

	Right	Wrong
1 The Köhlers went to Croatia by car. ______________________	☐	☐
2 They stayed at a campsite. ______________________	☐	☐
3 It rained a lot in Croatia. ______________________	☐	☐
4 Tom went surfing every day. ______________________	☐	☐
5 Tom spoke English a lot. ______________________	☐	☐
6 They only stayed on the island of Krk. ______________________	☐	☐

c) Back at school Tom writes an e-mail to Maria, the girl from Spain. He writes about their great holidays and his first days at school. Write Tom's e-mail into your exercise book.

Als Tom wieder zu Hause ist, schreibt er Maria aus Spanien eine E-Mail. Er schreibt über seine tollen Ferien und über seine ersten Tage in der Schule. Schreib Toms E-Mail in dein Heft.

[1] to hire a car = einen Leihwagen mieten
[2] to have a great view = eine tolle Aussicht haben
[3] still = immer noch

a) Look at the pictures and put them into the right order.

1

2

3

4

5

6

7

8

b) *Now tell the story in your own words. Write your story in the simple past and use linking words and time phrases. The box below can help you.*

Erzähle die Geschichte in eigenen Worten.
Schreib im simple past *und benutze* linking words *und Zeitangaben. Die untenstehende Box kann dir helfen.*

In the first night after his holidays, Tom had a dream about Maria. They were …

____

____

____

____

____

____

____

____

Remember:

linking words	**time phrases**
first	in the morning
then	in the
afternoon	
after that / afterwards	in the evening
next	at 7 o'clock
before	…
later	
but	
suddenly	
…	

a) *Ask your partner about the gaps in your chart and fill in the answers.*
Then answer your partner's questions.

Partner A:

Who?	What ... their last party?	How … go there?	What … do?	When … leave the party?
Anna	*her grandmother's 70th birthday*		*have nice dinner at a restaurant*	*10 pm*
Gemma		*on foot*		
Paul	*Mark's fancy dress party*[1]		*have a prize for the best costume and play party games*	*stay there on Friday night*
Mark		*by bike*		
You				
Your partner				

b) *Now swap your charts and check!*

c) *Do you remember the last party you went to? What was it like?*

[1] fancy dress party = Kostümparty

✂---

a) *Ask your partner about the gaps in your chart and fill in the answers.*
Then answer your partner's questions.

Partner B:

Who?	What ... their last party?	How … go there?	What … do?	When … leave the party?
Anna		*by car*		
Gemma	*Anna's garden party*		*have a barbecue*	*9 pm*
Paul		*by bus*		
Mark	*school's-out-party*		*dance a lot and sing karaoke*	*8 pm*
You				
Your partner				

b) *Now swap your charts and check!*

c) *Do you remember the last party you went to? What was it like?*

[1] fancy dress party = Kostümparty

Unit 2 – Überblick

KV 2.1 Scrambled words

Bei dieser Wortschatzübung entschlüsseln die S die Wörter und schreiben sie auf. Danach ordnen sie sie entsprechend der vorgegebenen Wortfelder. So üben und vertiefen die S nicht nur den neuen Wortschatz, sondern schulen auch ihre methodischen Fertigkeiten in Bezug auf das Vokabellernen.

KV 2.2 Information gap: Big, bigger, the biggest

Partnerarbeit: Mithilfe dieser KV lassen sich die Steigerungsformen regelmäßig gesteigerter und unregelmäßig gesteigerter Adjektive passiv festigen. Die S füllen die Leerstellen mit den passenden Zahlen und vergleichen ihre Lösungen mit dem Lösungsschlüssel.

KV 2.3 Who's the youngest of the three?

Die S vergleichen die drei vorgegebenen Steckbriefe. Dabei bilden sie die Steigerungsformen der Adjektive selbstständig und wenden sie im Zusammenhang an. Im Anschluss daran können die S den eigenen Steckbrief mit dem eines Partners vergleichen.

KV 2.4 Let's have a party!

Diese Übung kombiniert Wortschatz und Mengenangaben. Zunächst vervollständigen die S eine Einladung zu einer Party und erstellen anschließend eine passende Einkaufsliste.

KV 2.5 What are you going to be?

Diese Aufgabe zum Leseverstehen übt zunächst passiv die Verwendung des *going to-future*. Im zweiten Teil werden die S angeregt, den aktiven Umgang mit dem *going to-future* an einem selbst verfassten Text zu erproben. Hilfen für das Wortfeld finden die S im Dialogtext.

KV 2.6 At the party

In diesem Lückentext wird die Verwendung von *some* und *any* sowie deren Zusammensetzungen geübt. Inhaltlich greift der Text die Situation der Klassenparty auf und enthält einige der grammatikalischen Strukturen, die in Unit 2 schwerpunktmäßig behandelt werden.

KV Scrambled words

a) *All the words have something to do with fashion or food and drinks.*
Write down the correct words.
Alle Wörter haben etwas mit Mode oder Essen und Trinken zu tun. Schreib die richtigen Wörter auf.

1 titfuo - *outfit* ______
2 serds - ______
3 sichp - ______
4 damaonele - ______
5 ihfason - ______
6 tewess - ______
7 winachds - ______
8 anserrit - ______
9 olulperv - ______
10 ripscs - ______
11 limk - ______
12 osusretr - ______
13 cei marec - ______
14 laco - ______
15 strosh - ______
16 locetacho - ______
17 labelsab pac - ______
18 krits - ______
19 gorena ejicu - ______
20 stoob - ______

b) *Now put the words into the right box.*
Add more words you know about food and drink and fashion.
Ordne die Wörter den Kästen zu.
Du kannst weitere Wörter zu den Themen Essen und Trinken und Mode dazuschreiben.

Food and drink	Fashion
• ______	• *outfit*

Remember:

Wörter kannst du besser behalten, wenn du sie in **Wortgruppen** sammelst, z.B. in **Wortfamilien** (*to begin, beginning, beginner*), **Gegensatzpaaren** (*happy – sad*) oder, wie in dieser Übung, in **Wortfeldern**. Hierbei ordnest du die zu lernenden Wörter einem **Oberbegriff** (*group word*) zu.

Auch **Wortnetze** (*networks*) machen es dir leichter, Wörter zu behalten.

a) *Listen to your partner and write down* ***1*** *for the adjective (*for example: fast*),* ***2*** *for the comparative (*faster*) and* ***3*** *for the superlative (*the fastest*) in your table. Take turns.*

Hör dir die Sätze deines Partners an und schreib ***1*** *für jedes Adjektiv (z.B.* fast*),* ***2*** *für die Steigerungsform (*faster*) und* ***3*** *für den Superlativ (*fastest*) in deine Tabelle. Wechselt euch ab.*

Partner A:

	1	2	3	4
A	*Toby's car is* ***faster*** *than mine.*	*the friendliest =* ***3***	*Tokio Hotel is the best band in the world!*	
B	*Today the weather is very good.*			*Mrs Clark has the most beautiful smile.*
C	*I am taller than all the other children in my class.*		*I can understand John well, he's the best pupil in our English class.*	*This house is not bigger than mine!*
D		*Do you want to see the ugliest monster of the three?*		

✂---

a) *Listen to your partner and write down* ***1*** *for the adjective (*for example: fast*),* ***2*** *for the comparative (*faster*) and* ***3*** *for the superlative (*the fastest*) in your table. Take turns.*

Hör dir die Sätze deines Partners an und schreib ***1*** *für jedes Adjektiv (z.B.* fast*),* ***2*** *für die Steigerungsform (*faster*) und* ***3*** *für den Superlativ (*fastest*) in deine Tabelle. Wechselt euch ab.*

Partner B:

	1	2	3	4
A	*faster=**2***	*We are the* ***friendliest*** *people in the world!*		*When does this terrible rain stop?*
B		*This chocolate tastes better than the other one.*	*Don't take this way, it's the longest.*	
C		*When can we see Tom Cruise's new movie?*		
D	*This flower is more beautiful than the others in this garden.*		*Wait, this handbag is cheaper than the one you've got!*	*And you are the cleverest person in the world? Ha-ha!!!*

KV Who's the youngest of the three?

a) *Compare the three children and write five sentences about them.*
Use the information from the profiles. The adjectives in the box can help.

Vergleiche die drei Kinder und schreib fünf Sätze über sie. Benutz die Informationen aus den Steckbriefen. Die Adjektive im Kasten helfen dir.

Name:	Marc
Height:	1.55 m
Age:	11
Hobby:	swimming
Family:	2 sisters
Pets:	1 (a dog)

Name:	Linda
Height:	1.60 m
Age:	12
Hobby:	dancing
Family:	no brothers or sisters
Pets:	3 (a cat + two mice)

Name:	Toby
Height:	1.65 m
Age:	12
Hobby:	riding
Family:	1 brother
Pets:	2 (a horse + a cat)

tall • small • old • young • interesting • boring • how many • big

Example: *Linda is taller than Marc, but Toby is taller than the two/the tallest.*

1 ______________________________

2 ______________________________

3 ______________________________

4 ______________________________

5 ______________________________

b) *Now you! Fill in your own profile, then compare it with a partner's.*

Füll deinen eigenen Steckbrief aus. Vergleiche ihn dann mit dem eines Partners.

Name: ____________________

Height: ____________________

Age: ____________________

Hobby: ____________________

Family: ____________________

Pets: ____________________

1 ______________________________

2 ______________________________

3 ______________________________

4 ______________________________

5 ______________________________

a) *Anna, Linda and Marc are organising a party for their form.*
Fill in the missing information on the invitation.

Anna, Linda und Marc organisieren eine Party für ihre Klasse. Ergänze die fehlenden Informationen in der Einladung.

Invitation

It's party time!

We are going to have a ____________________

on ____________________________

at ___________

in _______________________.

We are going to have a best costume competition[1],

so dress up in your

_______________________________.

Come and enjoy

- ________________________________
- *best hot dogs and cocktails in town*
- *being together and having fun*

See you at the party!

Anna, Linda & Marc

great music and karaoke • 7 pm • most exciting costume • fancy dress party Friday • 5th September • our classroom

[1] best costume competition = Kostümwettbewerb

A few days before the party the three students talk about the food and drinks for the party. They have invited 25 students. They want to make hot dogs and lots of other things.

Ein paar Tage vor der Party reden die drei Schüler über Essen und Getränke für die Party. Sie haben 25 Klassenkameraden eingeladen. Sie wollen Hot Dogs und viele andere Sachen machen.

b) *Write the shopping list for them. The boxes below might help you.*

Schreib die Einkaufliste für die Schüler. Die Kästen unten können dir helfen.

Shopping list

- *13 bottles of coke*
- ______________________
- ______________________
- ______________________
- ______________________
- ______________________
- ______________________
- ______________________
- ______________________

How much / how many …
bottle(s) of
litre(s) of
jar(s) of
packet(s) of
kilo(s) of
carton(s) of
can(s) of
tin(s) of
bar(s) of

Food and drink
coke
lemonade
orange juice
rolls
sausages
mustard
crisps
chocolate
ketchup
potato salad

Tina, Toby and Peter have received an invitation for a fancy dress party[1]. Now they are talking about which costumes they are going to wear and what they are going to need for them.

Tina, Toby und Peter sind zu einer Kostümparty eingeladen. Sie reden über die Kostüme, die sie anziehen werden und was sie dafür brauchen.

***a)** Read the text:*

Tina: Hello Toby. Listen, aren't you invited to this party next Saturday too? What are you going to be ? I am still not sure about it.
Toby: I think I am going to wear the costume I have from the last fancy dress party, the clown costume. It's still very good, but my parents are going to buy me a new hat for it.
Peter: A clown, how boring is that!?! You are going to look very silly!
Toby: Hey, that isn't fair! What's your costume going to be like then?
Peter: It's a secret, but I am going to give you some hints: I am going to wear a lot of grey, my best friend George is going to be a part of it too, and we are going to have very big ears!
Tina: That's easy! You two are going to be an elephant!!!
Peter: That's right, cool, isn't it?
Toby: Well, OK, I am going to think about my costume again…
Tina: Toby, I've got an idea! We are going to wear the elephant costume and we are going to dress Peter like a monkey and that's not even a costume for him!
Peter: Haha, very funny! Anyway, it is going to be a great party, whatever you are.

***b)** Tick (✓) the right box. The letters behind the correct answer form a word from the text.*

The party is going to take place	on Monday	☐	a
	on Sunday	☐	f
	on Saturday	☐	c
Toby is going to	buy a new costume	☐	d
	borrow a costume	☐	e
	wear an old costume	☐	l
His parents are going to buy him	new trousers	☐	p
	a new hat	☐	o
	a new red nose	☐	i
Peter and George are going to be	an elephant	☐	w
	a monkey	☐	k
	a horse	☐	m
Peter	is not invited to the party	☐	t
	is looking forward to the party	☐	n
	doesn't like parties	☐	s

What's the word? ___ ___ ___ ___ ___

[1] fancy dress party = Kostümparty

b) *Imagine you are also invited to this party. What are you going to be? A clown? A monkey? An elephant? Write 5 sentences about your costume and remember to use the going to-future!*

Stell dir vor, du bist auch zur Party eingeladen. Als was wirst du dich verkleiden? Als Clown? Als Affe? Als Elefant? Schreib fünf Sätze über dein Kostüm. Denk daran, das going to-future *zu benutzen!*

1 ______________________________

2 ______________________________

3 ______________________________

4 ______________________________

5 ______________________________

Remember:

Das *going to-future* wird gebildet mit einer Form von *to be (am, are, is), going to* und dem Infinitiv des Verbs.
Man benutzt diese Zeitform für Absichten oder Pläne in der Zukunft, aber auch, wenn etwas sehr wahrscheinlich passieren wird, da es schon Anzeichen dafür in der Gegenwart gibt.

The children are talking to each other at the party. Fill in some, any, something, anything, somewhere …

Anna: Oh no. We haven't got ________________ hot dogs left. Hurry up, Linda, we need ________________ more. These hot dogs are the best in town. Everybody loves them.

Linda: OK, OK. I can go and make _______________. But are there enough orange juice and cola in the fridge, Marc?

Marc: Yes, everything is fine, ladies! This is going to be the best party in the world. Look! The people are having fun, they are dancing and laughing.

Anna: And most of the costumes are fantastic. ____________ children spent a lot of money on their costumes. But I think Peter and George's elephant costume is the best.

Marc: No, I don't think so. Tina's costume is much more exciting. She looks great in her short skirt and …

Linda: Oh, stop it, Marc! Have you seen Toby ____________________? He didn't look very happy in his costume.

Anna: He must be _______________________. I saw him a few minutes ago. He was talking to __________________ girls in very nice sixties outfits. They liked his clown costume a lot.

Marc: Hmmm, there he is – on the dance floor with the girls. He looks happy now. Why isn't ____________________________ dancing with me?

Linda: Poor Marc! Give me ______________________ to drink and help me with the hot dogs. Then we can go dancing.

Remember:

Some, somebody, something und *somewhere* verwendest du vor allem in bejahten Aussagesätzen.

Any, anybody, anything und *anywhere* verwendest du vor allem in verneinten Aussagesätzen und Fragen.

Unit 3 – Überblick

KV 3.1 Crossword: Animals

Diese Wortschatzübung dient der Festigung und Wiederholung des Wortschatzes zum Thema Tiere. Ein Lösungswort animiert zur Fertigstellung des Kreuzworträtsels.

KV 3.2 When this lesson ends …

Diese Übung festigt den Gebrauch des *will-future*, indem die S es in realitätsnahem Kontext schriftlich bilden.

KV 3.3 What will your do if …?

Anhand dieser Übung wird die Bildung der Konditionalsätze des Typs 1 geübt. Die S wählen aus zwei Möglichkeiten aus und formulieren, was sie unter der jeweiligen Bedingung tun werden.

KV 3.4 Our crazy teacher

An diesem Lückentext und der sich anschließenden Schreibaufgabe üben die S die Unterscheidung und Anwendung von Adjektiv und Adverb.

KV 3.5 TV – television

Diese Wortschatzübung festigt das Wortfeld zu TV und übt das Beschreiben fester Gewohnheiten. Um die Schreibaufgabe für schwächere S zu erleichtern, werden im ersten Teil die Wörter gesammelt, die beim anschließenden Schreiben des kurzen Textes verwendet werden sollen.

KV 3.6 Do you know what these animals need?

Diese Übung ist eine Ausgangsbasis und Ideenquelle für einen eigenen Text über ein Lieblings- oder Haustier und dessen Bedürfnisse. Als Vorentlastung liefert die KV im ersten Teil Sätze zu Tieren, die als zutreffend oder falsch bewertet werden müssen.

Look at the pictures and write down the names of the animals.

It's Monday morning and 13-year-old Toby is sitting in his classroom. The teacher, Mr Manning, is talking and writing words on the board.

Toby is bored. He takes out a piece of paper and starts making plans[1] for the future.

Imagine you are Toby. Write down his plans.

Stell dir vor, du bist Toby. Schreib seine Pläne auf.

When this lesson ends, I will eat a sandwich.

After school, I ______________________________

And then I ______________________________

When the summer holidays are here, I ______________________________

______________________________ and ______________________________

____

When I finish school ______________________________

____

____

and ______________________________

When I am thirty, I'll probably ______________________________

____

____

and ______________________________

Rrriiiiing!!!! The bell rings, Toby looks up and thinks: "Great, the lesson is over!!! No more planning. Now I can do all the things I want to do!"

[1] to make plans = Pläne machen

a) *What will you do if …? Choose one situation (✓) and form a sentence like this:*

Was wirst du tun, wenn …? Such dir eine Situation aus (✓) und bilde einen Satz:

good weather ☑
bad weather ☐

If the weather is good, I will go to the park and have a picnic there.

go to the zoo ☐
go to the cinema ☐

____

make a trip to London ☐
make a trip to Hawaii ☐

____

do my homework ☐
don't do my homework ☐

____

watch TV ☐
play a computer game ☐

____

meet my friend in town ☐
meet my friend at home ☐

____

have a Music lesson ☐
have an English lesson ☐

____

b) *Make a worksheet like this one for each other. Fill in your partner's worksheet.*

Entwirf ein ähnliches Arbeitsblatt für deinen Partner. Füll das Arbeitsblatt deines Partners aus.

KV Our crazy teacher

a) *Fill in the gaps. Be careful: sometimes you need an adjective and sometimes you need an adverb.*

Vervollständige den Lückentext. Aber Vorsicht: manchmal brauchst du ein Adjektiv und manchmal ein Adverb.

Mr. Funny is our ________________ (crazy) Music teacher. He always comes into our classroom in a __________________ (funny) way. He opens the door very _______________ (slow), and we only see his ____________________ (big) and _______________ (round) head. Then he looks at us __________________ (strange) and after that he comes in _____________________ (quick). He sits down on his chair ____________________ (careful) and he closes his eyes ____________________ (slow). Then he stands up again and starts to sing ______________________ (terrible). Mr. Funny can play the piano very ______________ (good), but his voice is really ______________________ (bad). We have to listen to his favourite song in every lesson. He sings so _______________________ (loud) that sometimes the teacher from the class next to ours knocks at the door______________________ (angry) and shouts: "Be ______________ (quiet). Stop that ___________________ (terrible) noise." But Mr. Funny thinks that he is a __________________ (wonderful) singer and he goes on and on and on … At first, we had to laugh about this ____________________ (strange) man, but now we think he is _____________________ (crazy).

b) *Not all the teachers are like Mr. Funny. Write down four sentences about your favourite teacher(s). Write down what they do and how they do things, what they look like etc. You can use the words in the box.*

Nicht alle Lehrer sind wie Mr. Funny. Schreib vier Sätze über deine/n Lieblingslehrer/in. Schreib auf, was sie tun und wie sie es tun, wie sie aussehen, usw. Benutze die Wörter im Kasten.

tall/small • teach • friendly • dark hair • write on the board • well prepared old/ young • speak/talk to the pupils • funny • explain sth. well/clearly interesting lessons • laugh/smile • fair • walk • clever • shout • cool

____

____

____

____

____

a) *Put more words about television into the network. Here are some ideas:*

Füge dem Netzwerk mehr Wörter zum Thema Fernsehen hinzu. Hier sind einige Ideen:

- places where you can watch ...
- people who work for …
- favourite food to eat when you watch …
- different kinds of programmes ...
- channels that you know ...
- how you feel when you watch …

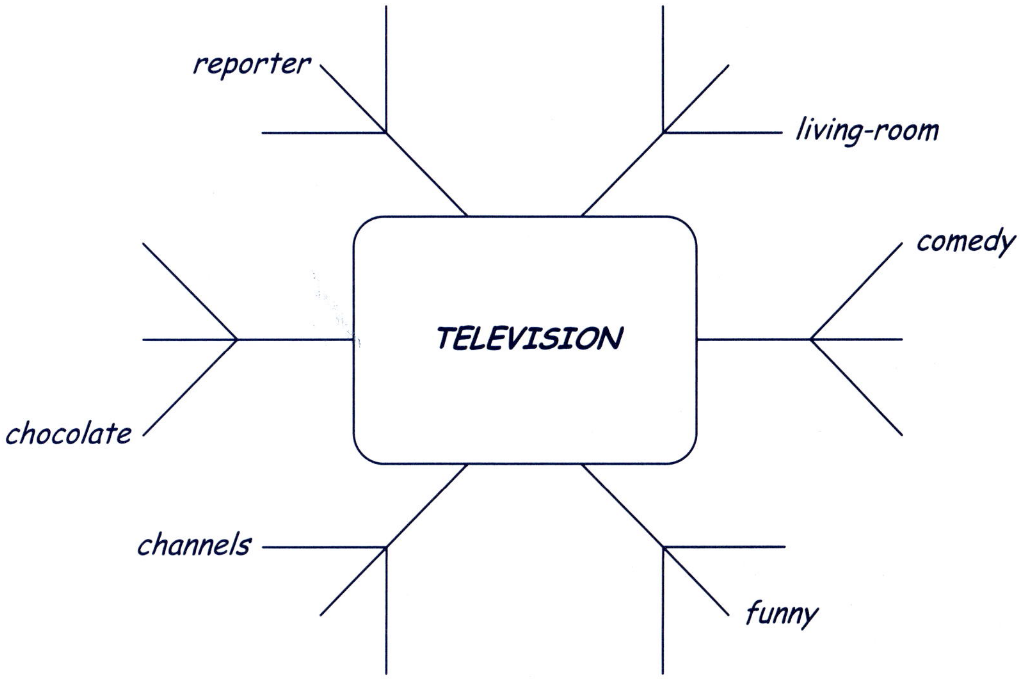

b) *Now you. Answer the following questions:*

1 When do you usually watch TV?
2 What do you like to see? Why?
3 What don't you watch? Why not?
4 Who do you watch TV with?
5 How much television do you watch every day/week?

KV Do you know what these animals need?

a) *Right or wrong? Read the following sentences and tick (✓) the right box. If you think a sentence is wrong, you can give the correct answer below.*

Richtig oder falsch? Lies die Sätze und hake (✓) das richtige Kästchen ab. Wenn du denkst, dass ein Satz falsch ist, berichtige ihn.

	Right	Wrong
1 Frogs live in or near the water.	☐	☐
2 They sleep at night.	☐	☐
3 Frogs are very good at dancing.	☐	☐
4 They can be very loud.	☐	☐
5 Hedgehogs have two legs.	☐	☐
6 They drink water.	☐	☐
7 Hedgehogs love milk, too!	☐	☐
8 They shouldn't eat bread, it's dangerous for them.	☐	☐
9 They eat food for pets.	☐	☐
10 You shouldn't touch them with gloves.	☐	☐

b) *Are you an animal expert or do you have a pet? What does it like/not like? How and where does it live? What does it eat? Write a text about it. You can add a picture of the animal you write about.*

Bist du ein Tierexperte oder hast du ein Haustier? Was mag es, was mag es nicht? Wie und wo lebt es? Was frisst es? Schreib einen kurzen Text. Du kannst ein Bild hinzufügen.

Unit 4 – Überblick

KV 4.1 Parts of the body

Diese Wortschatzübung dient der Festigung und Wiederholung des Wortschatzes zu *body parts, clothes, illnesses* und *injuries.*

KV 4.2 Word grid: Have you ever done this?

Diese KV festigt über mehrere Stationen (erkennen, aufschreiben, Partnerarbeit, Sätze bilden) den Gebrauch der *past participles.*

KV 4.3 Word order

Diese Übung dient der Wiederholung der Satzstruktur im Englischen (*S-V-O*). Hinzu kommt die in dieser Unit neu eingeführte Regel *place before time.* Die anschließende Partnerarbeit sorgt bei den S für ein stärkeres Bewusstsein für falsche und richtige Satzstrukturen, wenn sie ihre allein verfassten Texte Korrektur lesen.

KV 4.4 An e-mail from Wales

Die Schwerpunkte dieser Übung liegen auf dem Leseverstehen, dem Markieren und Entnehmen bestimmter Informationen aus einem Text und schließlich dem Schreiben mit weitgehend offenem Schreibauftrag.

KV 4.5 Can or may?

Diese KV dient der Einübung der Ersatzformen für *can* und *may* in der Vergangenheit und der Zukunft. Die Progression geht von einer Einsatzübung im Präsens zur Festigung über den getrennten Gebrauch der Zeiten bis zu einer Übung mit gemischten Zeiten.

KV 4.6 What happened?

Diese Übung dient der Wiederholung des *simple past* als Zeit für Berichte über Ereignisse. Die S beschreiben anhand der Bilder einen Unfallhergang im *simple past.* Dabei berichten sie zunächst in einer Art Dialog mit immer offeneren Fragen über den dargestellten Unfall. Anschließend können sie eine eigene Situation zeichnen, die sie anschließend in einem selbst verfassten Text beschreiben.

a) Write down the words for the parts of the body. If you want to, you can colour in the pictures.

Schreib die Wörter für die Körperteile auf. Wenn du willst, kannst du die Bilder ausmalen.

b) Do you remember the words for the children's clothes? Finish the sentences.

Erinnerst du dich an die Vokabeln für die Kleidung der Kinder? Beende die Sätze.

The girl is wearing ____.

The boy is wearing ____.

c) Find the eight illnesses and injuries in the word snake and write them down.

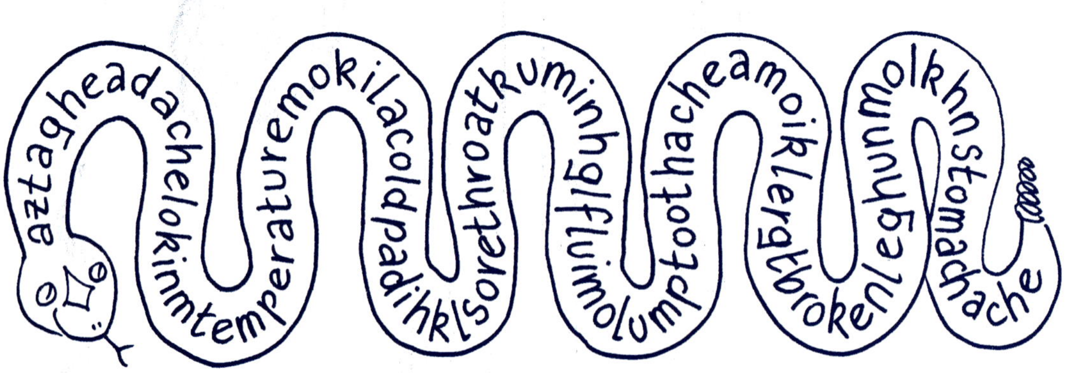

You can have a ____

____.

a) *Find the ten past participles in the grid.*

Finde die zehn Vergangenheitsformen.

m	d	c	o	o	k	e	d	n	p	a	q
e	e	i	o	l	m	j	u	e	d	d	b
t	k	l	s	w	h	v	n	t	b	e	k
d	a	r	p	u	m	d	k	t	a	h	r
d	r	o	p	p	e	d	l	i	y	c	t
o	s	s	r	b	n	u	o	r	f	t	n
p	h	a	d	a	o	i	p	w	z	a	o
p	a	b	a	s	d	k	k	l	u	w	l
t	f	o	e	v	o	o	p	b	d	j	l
u	t	t	r	a	v	e	l	l	e	d	m
w	s	e	f	h	u	b	s	l	v	t	b
a	o	w	p	s	d	g	k	l	o	a	o
c	l	z	n	a	w	r	q	o	m	b	t

b) *Write them down together with their infinitives.*

Schreib sie mit ihren Grundformen auf.

past participle	infinitive
met	*meet*

c) *Have you ever done this? Tick (√) yes or no.*

	me?		my partner?	
	yes	no	yes	no
travel to Wales	☐	☐	☐	☐
cook spaghetti	☐	☐	☐	☐
meet Brad Pitt	☐	☐	☐	☐
drop a glass	☐	☐	☐	☐
move to another town	☐	☐	☐	☐
lose a purse	☐	☐	☐	☐
write a poem	☐	☐	☐	☐
watch a scary movie	☐	☐	☐	☐
have a pet	☐	☐	☐	☐
read a magazine on clothes	☐	☐	☐	☐

d) *Now ask your partner the questions and tick (✓) the right answer.*

Partner A: Have you ever travelled to Wales?
Partner B: Yes I have. / No, I haven't.

e) *Write ten sentences about your answers and your partner's answers. Use the information from c).*

Schreib zehn Sätze zu deinen Antworten und denen deines Partners. Benutz die Informationen aus c).

Remember:

I / you / we / they	+	*have*	+	participle
ich / du / wir / sie	+	haben	+	Partizip
he / she / it	+	*has*	+	participle
er / sie / es	+	hat	+	Partizip

You	***Your partner***
I have ...	*He/she has ...*

Do you remember the correct word order in English sentences?
It's different from German word order, so be careful!

Remember:

S-V-O, das heißt	*subject*	*verb*	*object*
	I	*like*	*ice-cream.*
	We	*are*	*in Chester.*
	Toby	*likes*	*Stella.*

Außerdem gilt: *place before time*, das heißt Orts- vor Zeitangabe

We'll go to Chester tomorrow.
I went to Berlin last year.

Aber: Du kannst die Zeitangabe auch an den Satzanfang stellen, wenn du diese besonders betonen möchtest. Mit der Ortsangabe kannst du nicht so verfahren.

Tomorrow we'll go to Chester.
Last year I went to Berlin.

a) *Form sentences:*

1 ride / to school / Toby and Tina / their bikes / every morning

____

2 went / to the zoo / we / at the weekend

____

3 hate / Maths tests / I / a lot

____

4 my father / can / the trumpet / play

____

5 went / this year / they / on holiday to Spain

____

6 this game / you / today / cannot win

____

b) *It's puzzle time! Choose a partner. Write down sentences on a piece of paper, cut them into pieces and shuffle[1] them. Your partner has to put your sentences into the correct order. Then swap.*

Puzzle: Such dir einen Partner. Schreibt Sätze auf ein Blatt Papier, schneidet sie auseinander und mischt sie. Dein Partner muss deine Sätze in die richtige Reihenfolge bringen. Dann könnt ihr tauschen.

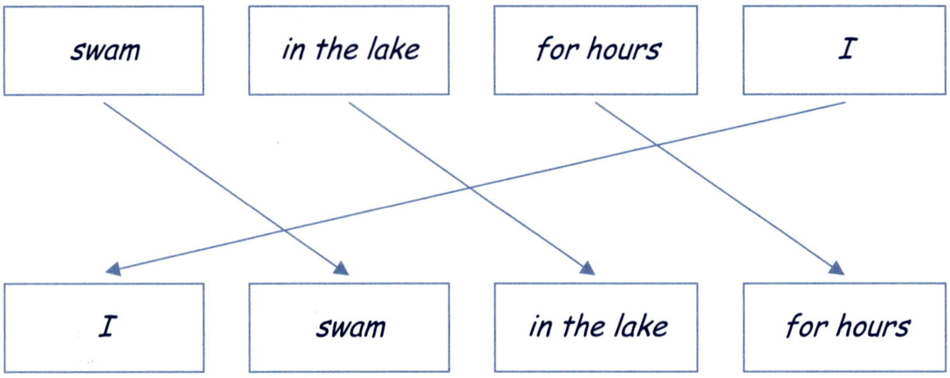

[1] to shuffle = mischen

Heidi, a girl from Hamburg, is on holiday in Wales with a group of young people. She is doing a surfing course. She writes the following e-mail from an internet café to her American friend Susan.

a) *Read the e-mail and mark the phrases that you can use in e-mails, chats or text messages (SMS).*

Lies die E-Mail und markiere die Ausdrücke, die du in E-Mails, Chats oder SMS verwenden kannst.

Send Cut Copy Save Cancel Print Tools Attach Priority

To: Susan.Miller@newyork-ny.com

CC:

Subject: **Yeah – surfing is great**

Hi Susan,

It's me from the country of green hills and sheep. Does this sound boring to you? It's not! lol

I've been in Wales for four days now. It's been fantastic! :)
We stay at a camp-site close to the beach. At night I can even hear the sea, which is great. The landscape is beautiful too. There are green fields with lots of sheep, high cliffs and the blue sea with big waves. You won't believe it, but I've already seen some seals. =o

The group is great. There are many really nice people from all over Europe. I'm in a tent with Lisa, a girl from London. She's already told me a lot about London. It must be an exciting place. She's invited me to come over next year. So I'll be in Britain's capital next summer. Isn't that exciting?

But surfing is the best. :))) It's great fun. My first surfing lessons were ok. Surfing looks easy, but it's really difficult. Just standing on the board is very hard. But Nick, my surfing instructor[1], says I'm doing fine. He must know, he is the best surfer in the world, I think. :-D And he's so sweet ...

The weather is really bad today, it's raining and raining. So no surfing today :(
2morrow we're going to make a trip to Cardiff - the capital of Wales. Shopping time!

Cu!

Heidi

b) *In her e-mail Heidi uses special symbols. Match the symbol with their meanings.*

In ihrer E-Mail benutzt Heidi spezielle Symbole. Ordne die Symbole ihrer Bedeutung zu.

:)	big smile
:)))	see you
:(	tomorrow
:-D	sad, bad
2morrow	laughing out loud
lol	very big smile
o=	surprise
cu	smile

[1] surfing instructor = Surflehrer

c) Now find a title for every paragraph of the e-mail.

1st paragraph: *Wales is fantastic*

2nd paragraph: ______________________________

3rd paragraph: ______________________________

4th paragraph: ______________________________

5th paragraph: ______________________________

d) Answer the following questions on the text.

1 Where does Heidi stay?

____

2 What does Heidi like about the landscape?

____

3 What does Heidi like most in her holidays? Why?

____

____

4 What do you get to know about Nick?

____

____

5 What is Heidi going to do next summer?

____

e) Would you like to travel to Wales? Would you like to learn how to surf? Why/why not?

____

____

____

____

____

____

____

____

a) *Put the right word into the gap.*

Setze das richtige Wort in die Lücke ein.

1 I ___*can*___ count up to 100 in English.

2 Mum says, I ____________________ watch TV until 10 o'clock in the evening.

3 Our car _________________ (not) drive more than 120 km/h, it is very old.

4 At schools today, our teachers ___________________ (not) hit us.

b) *Yesterday… (simple past) Remember to use* to be allowed to *or* to be able to.

1 … we ___*weren't allowed*_________ (not) to stay up late, the next day was a school day.

2 … our dog __________________ (not) go to the park, her leg was broken.

3 … our mum was very nice. She said we __________________ sleep late.

c) *Tomorrow … (will-future)*

1 … our team ____*will be able to*______ win the game, because the other team is very bad.

2 … you __________________ see the sum again, because the clouds will be gone by then.

3 … he __________________ (not) swim with me in the pool, because he hurt his foot.

d) *Attention! Mixed tenses. Watch out for signal words, they are underlined.*

Achtung, nun sind die Zeiten gemischt. Achte auf die unterstrichenen Signalwörter.

Tina: Hi Simon. Nice to see you. ___________ you help me? I will have a party tomorrow.

Simon: Of course. ___________ I come too?

Tina: Yes, but you ___________ also bring a friend if you like.

Simon: Good. So how ___________ I help you?

Tina: <u>Tomorrow</u> I _______________ (not) play loud music, so ___________ you bring your guitar?

Simon: Yes, what else ___________ I do?

Tina: Well, I _______________ (not) buy crisps <u>yesterday</u>, because the shops were closed, ___________ you help me buy some <u>now</u>?

Simon: Yes, ___________ I do something else for you?

Tina: I think that's all. But I _______________ (not) think clearly anymore, there are so many things to remember. I probably forgot something.

Simon: Don't worry, nobody ___________ remember everything.

a) *There was an accident on Church Street. You saw everything, so a policeman asks you questions.*

Auf der Church Street ist ein Unfall passiert. Du hast alles gesehen und wirst von einem Polizisten befragt.

Useful words and phrases:
stop sign • to crash into • to fall down on sth. • to hurt sth. • broken leg

Policeman: Good morning, did you see the accident?

You: ____

Policeman: Very good, I would like to ask you some questions about it. Which street was the man on the bike on before the accident happened? And where was the woman in the car?

You: ____

____

Policeman: Ok, so what happened then?

You: ____

____

____

____

Policeman: Thank you very much. You helped us a lot. Goodbye!

b) *Now you! Draw two pictures showing the situation before and after an accident. Then write a report for the police about it. Remember to use the simple past.*

Mal zwei Bilder, die die Situation vor und nach einem Unfall zeigen. Schreib einen Bericht für die Polizei. Denk daran, das simple past *zu benutzen.*

Unit 5 – Überblick

KV 5.1 Town and country

Diese Wortschatzübung dient der Festigung und Wiederholung des Wortschatzes zu Örtlichkeiten in der Stadt und auf dem Land. Darüber hinaus üben die S in einer Schreibaufgabe, die eigene Meinung zu begründen.

KV 5.2 Shopping in the city

Ziel dieser KV ist die Festigung der *question tags* in einem Dialog. Diese Textform wurde gewählt, weil die Frageanhängsel meist in der gesprochenen Sprache vorkommen.

KV 5.3 Mind map: Your town

Bei dieser Schreibaufgabe verfassen die S einen eigenen Text zum Thema *Your town*, nachdem sie zur Vorbereitung eine Mindmap vervollständigt haben. Für den Text werden Tipps zu Gestaltung und Aufbau gegeben. Für leistungsschwächere S stehen Worthilfen bereit.

KV 5.4 Irregular verbs

Gegen Ende des Halbjahres werden in diesen Übungen noch einmal spielerisch die unregelmäßigen Verbformen wiederholt und gefestigt.

KV 5.5 A very hard week in the life of Jenny Brown

Der Schwerpunkt dieser KV liegt auf dem Einsatz der Zeiten in ihrem jeweiligen Verwendungskontext. Dabei dienen Kalender und Bildimpulse als visuelle Vertiefungs- bzw. Erinnerungsmöglichkeiten. Im Anschluss erfolgt eine Übung mit gemischten Zeiten. Hier erschließen die S aus dem jeweiligen Kontext, welche Zeit sie verwenden müssen.

KV 5.6 Can you find the way to the rocket?

Ziel dieser KV ist die Wiederholung des *will-future* und des *going to-future*. Der Schwerpunkt liegt auf der Unterscheidung der Anwendungsbereiche beider Formen. Dabei müssen sich die S für einen Weg entlang der Kreuzchen entscheiden.

a) *Write down the English words for the places in town.*

b) *Now say what you can buy or do at these places.*

Nun sage, was man dort kaufen oder machen kann.

At the supermarket I can buy food and drinks.

5.1 KV Town and country

c) Write down the English words for the places in the country.

***d)** Say in a few sentences where you would like to live – in a town or in the country. Say why or why not. The phrases in the box can help you.*

Beschreibe in ein paar Sätzen, wo du gerne wohnen möchtest – in der Stadt oder auf dem Land. Begründe deine Meinung. Die Phrasen im Kasten können dir dabei helfen.

go shopping in a big department store • enjoy the quiet life • go to the cinema and watch a film • go for a nice walk • I'd like to live in … • because it's nice • that's why …

Remember:

Frageanhängsel werden häufig in der gesprochenen Sprache verwendet. Man verwendet sie, um vom Gesprächspartner Zustimmung zu bekommen.

Frageanhängsel bestehen aus einem Hilfsverb (*is, are, have, ...*) und einem Personalpronomen (*I, you, he, they, ...*). Ist der Aussagesatz bejaht, wird das Frageanhängsel verneint. Ist der Satz verneint, wird das Frageanhängsel bejaht.

You like to eat fish, don't you?
We don't need to clean the classroom, do we?

a) *Add the correct question tag after each sentence.*

Füge für jeden Satz das entsprechende Frageanhängsel hinzu.

Tina and Toby are on a shopping tour in Bristol. They have seen many things and Toby is tired. Tina wants to look at more clothes because she needs a dress for a party next weekend. Now they are walking along St Nicholas Market …

Tina: Hey Toby, stop! I want to look at this shop window. You're very tired, _______________?

Toby: Of course I am. We've been walking around town for hours now. And you don't want to stop, ____________?

Tina: No, I don't. I need a nice dress! How do you like this one? It's nice, ____________?

Toby: Yes, it's alright. But what about the blue one you've got at home? It's still cool, ____________? You can wear it to the party, _______________?

Tina: No, I can't! I've already worn it at the last party. You don't mind if I try this one on, ____________?

Toby: Fine. There's a chair and some biscuits, great!

Tina: You won't eat too many, ____________? We are going to have lunch with Jack and Ashley in 30 minutes.

Toby: Alright. But I can eat a lot, you know that, _______________? Hurry up and put on the dress, it could be the one, _______________?

Tina: You are making fun of me, _______________? But you're right, I like it a lot, give me two minutes.

10 minutes later: Toby has eaten all the biscuits. After he has finished the last one, he looks around … no Tina … He gets up from his chair and calls Tina's name. No answer, wait, there's a little voice from behind the curtain[1] …

Toby: Tina? It's you, ____________?

Tina: Yes, it's me, help me please! I got stuck[2] in the dress and I can't take it off!

Toby: Well, then we've finally found your dress, _______________?

[1] curtain = Vorhang
[2] to get stuck = feststecken

KV Mind map: Your town

a) *Make a mind map about your town. Put the name of your town into the box in the middle of the mind map. Use as many words and phrases as you can. Here are some ideas:*

Entwickle eine Mindmap zu deiner Stadt. Setze den Namen des Ortes in die Mitte. Verwende so viele Wörter und Ausdrücke, wie du kannst. Hier sind einige Anregungen:

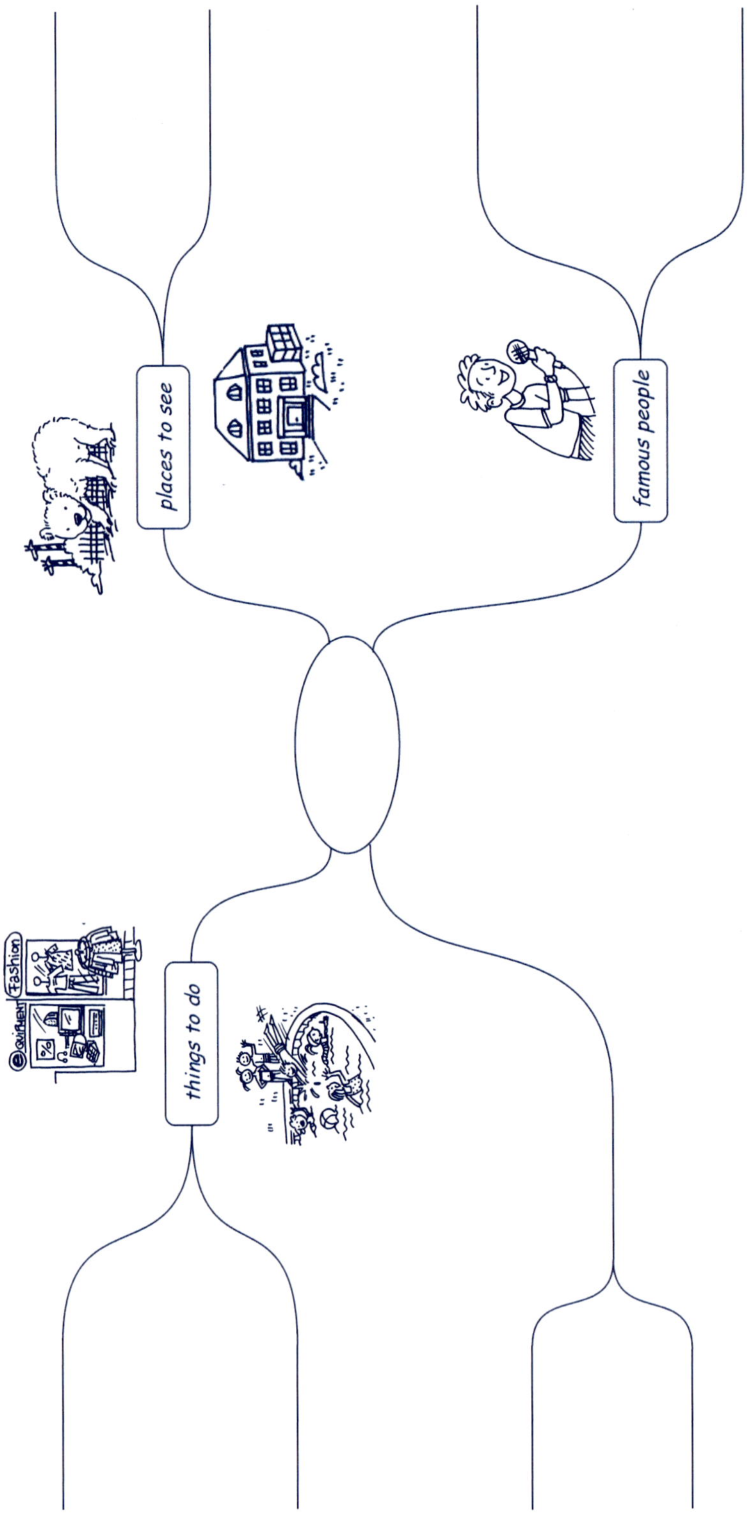

b) *Now write a text about your town. Use your ideas from the mind map and the phrases from the box. Remember: a text has a beginning, a middle and an end.*
Don't forget to write a good ending (for example, how you like your town).

Schreibe nun einen Text über deine Stadt. Verwende dabei deine Ideen aus der Mindmap und die Phrasen aus dem Kasten. Denk daran, dass ein Text eine Einleitung, einen Hauptteil und einen Schluss hat.
Vergiss nicht, ein gutes Ende zu finden (z.B. wie dir deine Stadt gefällt).

visit • see • go to • to look at • get information (about) • climb • walk
take a tour • learn about history • museum • castle • church • park
restaurant • have a picnic • have lunch • have dinner • have an ice-cream

c) *Look at your text again. Are your ideas connected? Did you use linking words like* before, then, next, after that*? If you didn't, please work on your text again and put some in.*
It helps the reader to understand your text much better.

Schau dir deinen fertigen Text noch einmal an. Hast du deine Ideen miteinander verbunden? Wenn nicht, überarbeite deinen Text erneut und setze verbindende Wörter ein, denn sie helfen dem Leser, deinen Text besser zu verstehen.

a) *Can you find all the 12 verbs in the snake? Write them down, then add their simple past forms.*

Kannst du alle 12 Verben in der Wortschlange finden? Schreibe sie zusammen mit ihren simple past-Formen auf.

infinitive	simple past
grow	*grew*

b) *Now fill in the past participles of the verbs.*

Trage nun die Partizipien der Verben in das Kreuzworträtsel ein.

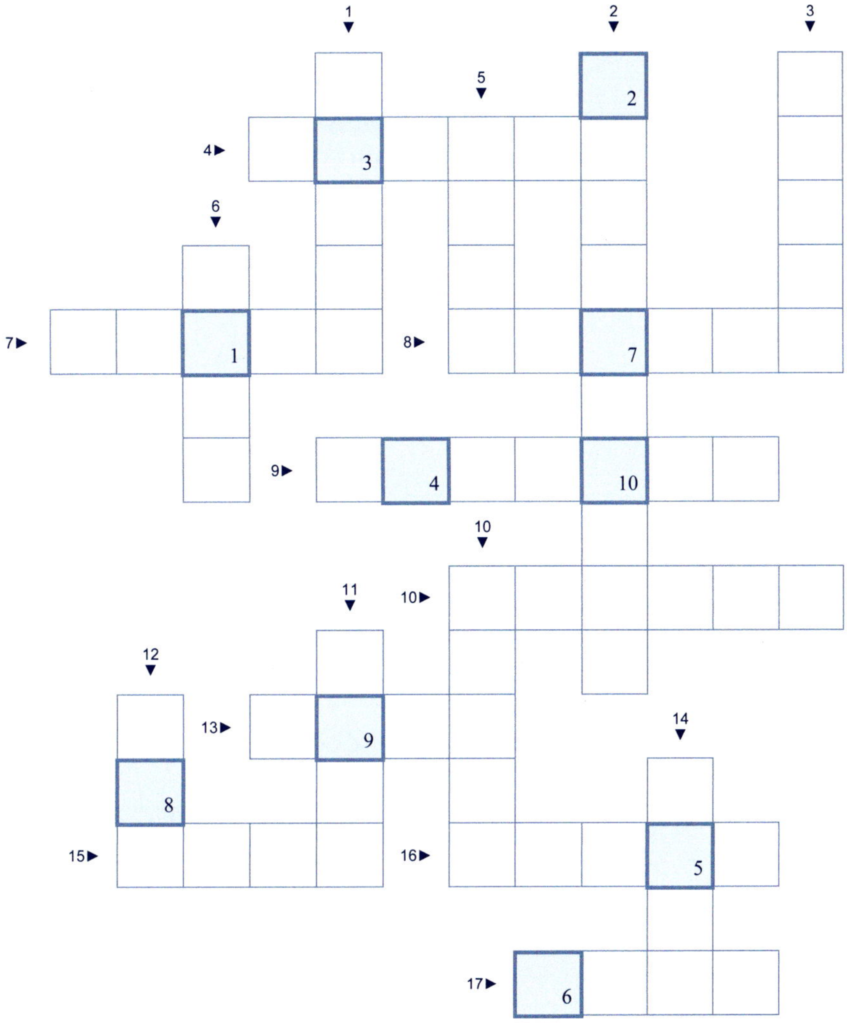

Across:

4 fall
7 fly
8 throw
9 write
10 speak
13 make
15 tell
16 take
17 go

Down:

1 eat
2 understand
3 give
5 lose
6 come
10 sleep
11 say
12 meet
14 be

	1	2		3	4	5		6	7	8	9	10	
Solution: y													!

5.5 KV A very hard week in the life of Jenny Brown

Jenny Brown is the singer of the band "The Jumping Monkeys". Last Saturday they had their first concert at a youth club near her school. The week before the concert was very hard …

a) *Look at Jenny's calendar and fill in the right form of the verb in the simple past.*

Schau dir Jennys Kalender an und fülle anschließend die Lücken in den Sätzen 1-6 aus. Benutze das simple past.

Monday, 7th April

make posters for concert

Tuesday, 8th April

meet band at 3pm
have rehearsal at 6pm

Wednesday, 9th April

Thursday, 10th April

talk to reporter from school magazine (at 4pm)

Friday, 11th April

rehearsal in the evening

argue with my parents ☹

Saturday, 12th April

CONCERT at 8pm

Sunday, 13th April

1 Last Monday Jenny ______________________ (have to) make posters for the concert.

2 On Tuesday at 3pm she ______________________ (meet) her band because they had to talk about their outfits for the concert.

3 They ______________________ (have) a rehearsal at 6pm on the same day.

4 Two days later Jenny ______________________ (talk to) a reporter from their school magazine. He wanted to do an interview with her.

5 After their very long rehearsal on Friday evening Jenny ____________________ (argue) with her parents. They were angry because she came home so late that evening.

6 On Saturday night the concert ______________________ (begin) at 8pm. When the concert was over she ______________________ (be) very happy because everybody liked their show.

b) *Look at the pictures and fill in the right form of the verb in the present perfect.*

Schau dir die Bilder an und fülle anschließend die Lücken in den Sätzen 1-6 aus. Verwende das present perfect.

1 Mike ____________________ (paint) a picture. Now he can put it on the wall.

2 His sister Helen ____________________ (finish) her homework.

She can listen to her new CD now.

3 Mike's mum ____________________ (do) the shopping for the weekend.

Now she can read her exciting book.

4 John, Mike's friend, ____________________ (repair[1]) his bike.

So now he can ride it to Mike's place.

---

[1] (to) repair = reparieren

c) **Extra** *Simple past or present perfect? Fill in the right tense of the verb. Watch out for signal words!*

Simple past *oder* present perfect? *Verwende die richtige Zeit in den Lücken. Achte auf Signalwörter!*

1 I can't come to your party tonight, because I ____________________ (not finish) my homework yet.

2 My parents ____________________ (get married) in 1990.

3 Last year we ____________________ (go) on our holiday to Portugal.

4 Wow, that sounds great. I ____________________ (never be) there before.

5 ____________________ you ever ____________________ (read) an English book?

6 Yesterday we ____________________ (go) on a trip to Berlin. That ____________________ (be) very interesting.

7 I ____________________ (start) to learn English two years ago.

8 Helen is so hungry. She ____________________ (not have) dinner yet.

9 I ____________________ (always want) to visit London. I ____________________ (heard) so many exciting stories about this city.

10 We ____________________ (go) to the cinema last night and ____________________ (watch) the new film with Brad Pitt.

Remember:

simple past	***present perfect***
Verwende das *simple past* bei • bestimmtem Zeitpunkt in der Vergangenheit • Bericht über Vergangenes (z.B. Geschichte erzählen)	Verwende das *present perfect* wenn es wichtig ist • <u>dass</u> jemand etwas getan hat / etwas geschehen ist (Zeitpunkt unwichtig) • dass die Handlung Auswirkungen auf die Gegenwart oder Zukunft hat
Signalwörter, die einen bestimmten Zeitpunkt angeben, sind z.B.: yesterday last summer, last year, last Monday three weeks ago in 2005	**Signalwörter, die unbestimmte Zeitangaben machen, sind z.B.:** already – schon, bereits just – (gerade) eben never – (noch) nie not … yet – noch nicht ever? – jemals? / schon mal? yet? – schon?

Remember:

Das ***going to-future*** benutzt du, wenn du über feste Absichten und Pläne für die Zukunft sprechen willst. Es wird gebildet aus einer Form von *to be (am/are/is)* und dem Infinitiv.

Das ***will-future*** benutzt du, wenn du ausdrücken willst, was in der Zukunft geschehen wird. Auch Vermutungen und Vorhersagen kannst du mit *will-future* ausdrücken. Zeitangaben sind *tomorrow, next month, soon, in a few weeks* und andere. Gebildet wird diese Zeit mit *will* und dem Infinitiv.
Wenn du eine verneinte Form verwenden willst, heißt es *will not*, oder kurz *won't*.

a) *Can you help the three little astronauts? They need to get to their rocket. Draw a line along the stars in the boxes and find the right way!*

Kannst du den drei kleinen Astronauten helfen? Sie müssen zu ihrer Rakete gelangen. Zeichne eine Linie entlang der Kreuze in den Kästchen und finde den richtigen Weg!

***will-* future?**	***going to-* future?**	The future is very exciting. You don't know what will happen next. But if you make plans, you know what you want to do with your time.
X	X	Maybe you ________________ (be) an astronaut.
X	X	Or you ________________ (live) in another country. Who knows?
X	X	Well, some do! First they ______________________ (finish) school.
X	X	Then they ________________ (go) to university.
X	X	And then? Nobody knows what ________________ (happen) next.
X	X	Often people want to know more about the future. They go to a fortune teller and he or she tells them more about their future. He or she might say: "Next year you ________________ (be) a millionaire!"
X	X	Or the fortune teller may talk about their family: "Next month your brother ________________ (win) a ticket for a pop concert!"
X	X	Whatever people tell you, the future ________________ (come).

Unit 6 – Überblick

KV 6.1 Can you tell me the way please?

Anhand dieser KV üben die S noch einmal Techniken zur Wegbeschreibung und zur genauen Beschreibung eines Standortes.

KV 6.2 What's happening outside?

Diese Übung dient der Wiederholung und Festigung des *present progressive.* Hier wird den S deutlich, dass das *present progressive* nicht nur für das verwendet wird, was gerade im Moment passiert, sondern auch für die Beschreibung von Bildern bzw. Szenen, die man beobachtet.

KV 6.3 What were the students doing?

Hier wiederholen und festigen die S das *past progressive,* indem sie zunächst ein Bild beschreiben und danach einen Text zu einer Situation aus ihrer eigenen Lebenswirklichkeit schreiben.

KV 6.4 Who, which or that?

Diese Lückentextübung festigt die korrekte Anwendung der Relativpronomen *who, which, whose* und *that.* Am Ende der KV stehen zur Erinnerung die Regeln zur Verwendung der Relativpronomen, die die S selbst vervollständigen.

KV 6.5 Let's play a game

Der Schwerpunkt dieser KV liegt auf der Festigung von Relativsätzen. Übungsform ist ein Spiel, das dem „Schiffe versenken" ähnelt.

KV 6.6 A night at school

Diese KV dient der Festigung der Verwendung von *mustn't* und *needn't* sowie der positiven Formen der Hilfsverben. Thematisch wird die Übung eingebunden in die Planung einer Klassenaktivität, für die Regeln abgesprochen werden müssen.

a) *Look at the map and answer the following questions. Be as clear as you can be.*

Schau dir den Stadtplan an und beantworte die folgenden Fragen. Sei so klar wie möglich.

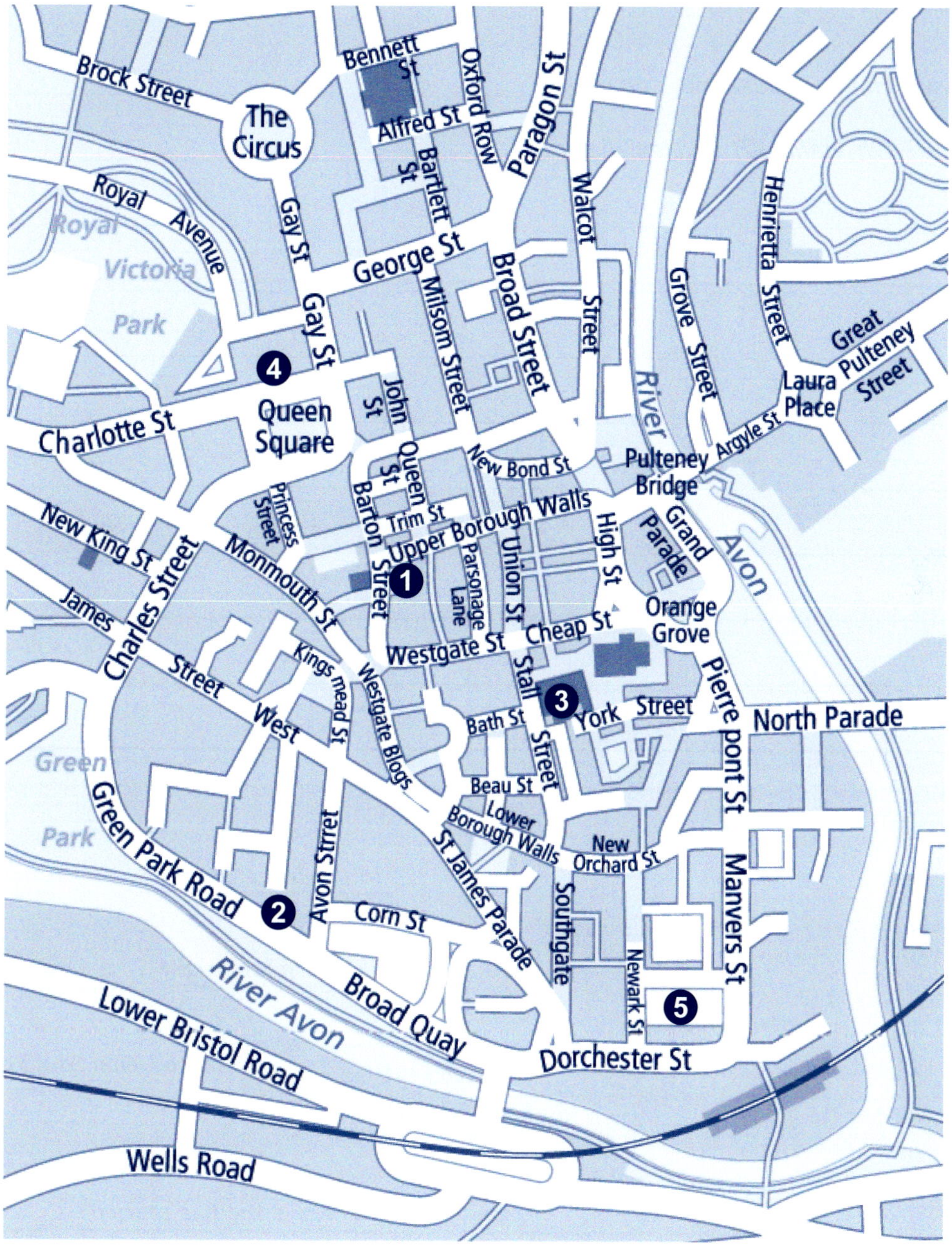

❶ hospital ❷ kindergarten ❸ Roman baths ❹ cinema ❺ bus station

Where's the hospital? ______________________________

Where's the kindergarten? ______________________________

Where are the Roman Baths? ______________________________

Where's the cinema? ______________________________

6.1 KV Can you tell me the way please?

b) *You are standing in front of the hospital. A tourist wants to know the way to the bus station. Write down the dialogue between you and the tourist. The mind map can help you.*

Du stehst vor dem Hospital. Ein Tourist fragt dich nach dem Weg zum Busbahnhof. Schreib den Dialog zwischen dir und dem Touristen auf.

Tourist: *Hello, excuse me, can you* ______________________________ *?*

You: *Oh, hello. Of course, I can.* ______________________________

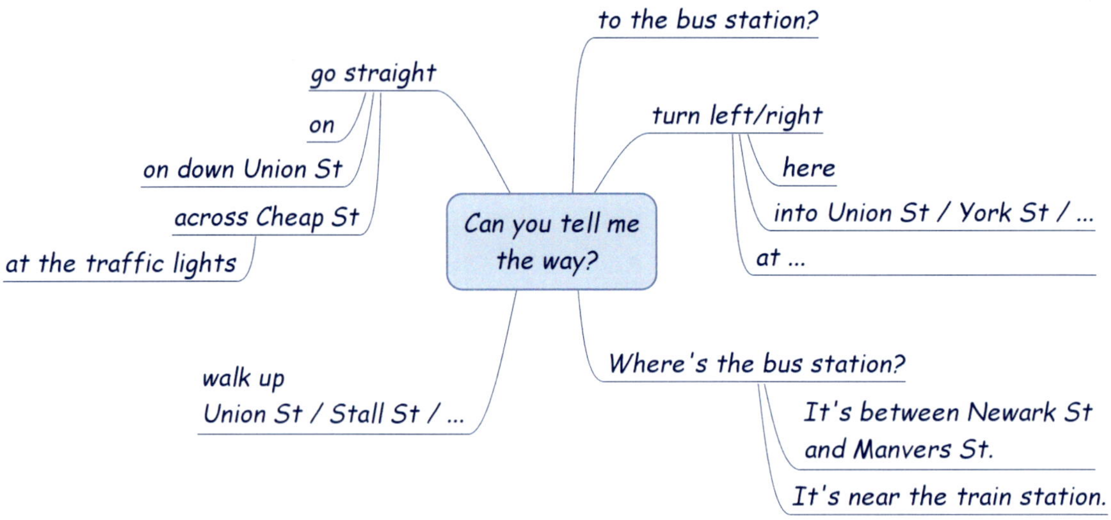

c) *Tell your partner where you are. Describe a way to another place. Your partner looks at the map and guesses the right place.*

Sag deinem Partner, wo du dich befindest. Beschreibe einen Weg zu einem anderen Ort. Dein Partner schaut auf den Plan und errät den richtigen Ort.

It's summertime and the sun is shining! But you're at home in your room because you have a cold and can't go outside. So you're looking out of the window instead. What do you see? The words in the box can help you.

Es ist Sommer und die Sonne scheint! Aber du bist zuhause, weil du eine Erkältung hast und nicht nach draußen kannst. Deshalb schaust du aus dem Fenster. Was siehst du? Die Wörter im Kasten können dir helfen.

take a walk • ride a bike • make a picnic • sleep • eat • drink • read
walk the dog • drive a car • take a break • have lunch • play cards • run

a) *Look at the picture and describe what the students were doing. Use the words in the box.*

Schau dir das Bild an und beschreibe, was die Schüler gerade machen. Benutze die Wörter im Kasten.

draw pictures • stand on chairs • listen to music • read magazines
eat sandwiches • do homework • talk to each other

When Mrs Smith came into the classroom, Peter was ______________________

b) *Think of your class. What were your classmates doing when your teacher came into your classroom yesterday or last week?*

Denk an deine eigene Klasse. Was haben deine Klassenkameraden gerade gemacht, als euer Lehrer gestern oder letzte Woche in den Klassenraum kam?

6.4 KV Who, which or that?

Mr Watson is the presenter of the quiz show. 'Do you know …?' Yesterday, he didn't have enough time to prepare the questions for the show. Can you help him?

Mr Watson ist Moderator der Quiz-Sendung 'Do you know?' Gestern hatte er nicht genug Zeit, um seine Fragen vorzubereiten. Kannst du ihm helfen?

a) *Put the correct relative pronouns into the gaps. When you use that, please enter who/which too.*

Trage das entsprechende Relativpronomen in die Lücken ein. Möchtest du that *verwenden, dann schreibe bitte auch noch* who/which *dazu.*

1 What is the name of the first of the three ducks ______________________ uncle is Donald Duck?

2 Can you tell me the name of an animal ______________________ lives in Australia?

3 I want to know the family name of the actor ______________________ plays James Bond?

4 What is the family name of the author ______________________ wrote the Harry Potter novels?

5 What is the name of the British capital ______________________ starts with an L?

b) *Can you answer the presenter's questions? Put them into the crossword puzzle:*

1 and **4** across;
2, **3** and **5** down

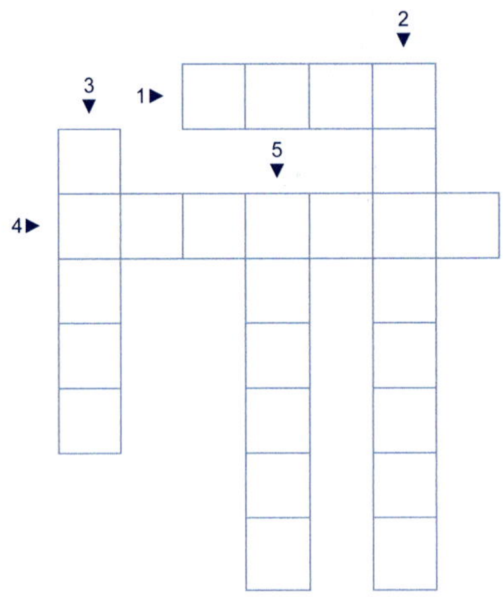

c) *Now that you practised where to put who, which, whose and that, can you complete these rules?*

Nachdem du nun die Verwendung der Relativpronomen geübt hast, kannst du diese Regeln ergänzen?

In relative clauses you …

… use ____________ for people

… use *which* for ____________

… can use ____________ for people and ____________

… use *whose* for ____________ but also for ____________.

In German, *whose* means ____________ or ____________.

Whose is always followed by a noun.

Rules for the game:

1. *Play this game with a partner (or in a group).*
2. *Make circles around five words in your grid.*
   Your partner is not allowed to see your grid.
3. *Try to guess your partner's words without saying the word.*
   You must describe it with a relative clause.
4. *If you describe a word that your partner has marked you win a point*
   and your partner must cross this word out.
5. *The partner who has guessed all the words first is the winner.*
6. *Write down the points on this chart:*

plane

~~**plane**~~

1. *Spiel dieses Spiel mit einem Partner (oder in einer Gruppe).*
2. *Kreise fünf Wörter in deiner Tabelle ein. Dein Partner darf deine Tabelle nicht sehen.*
3. *Versuch, die Wörter deines Partners zu erraten, ohne das Wort zu sagen. Beschreib es mit einem Relativsatz.*
4. *Wenn du ein Wort beschreibst, das dein Partner eingekreist hat, bekommst du einen Punkt und dein Partner muss das Wort durchstreichen.*
5. *Derjenige, der zuerst alle Wörter errät, ist der Gewinner.*
6. *Schreibt euren Punktestand in dieser Tabelle auf:*

Partner A	**Partner B**

Partner A: Your word describes something that can fly in the air.

Partner B: Oh, you're talking about the word 'plane' in A1.

Yes, I've circled it. → *Partner A gets a point.*

No, I haven't circled it. → *Partner A doesn't get a point.*
Partner B asks the next question.

Remember:

Relative clauses

Mit Relativsätzen kannst du genauer erklären, wen oder was du meinst.

who → steht für Personen: *The woman who is wearing the red skirt is Mrs Miller.*

which → steht für Dinge (und Tiere): *The red building which you can see over there is our school.*

that → kann für Personen und Dinge stehen

Partner A	1	2	3	4
A	plane	doctor	elephant	December
B	fireman	fish	actor	shop assistant
C	teacher	clock	cat	friend
D	dog	student	clown	budgie
E	table	board	classmate	cinema

Partner A	1	2	3	4
A	plane	doctor	elephant	December
B	fireman	fish	actor	shop assistant
C	teacher	clock	cat	friend
D	dog	student	clown	budgie
E	table	board	classmate	cinema

Mr Jenkins and his form are planning to spend a night at their school reading stories to each other. He wants to make rules with his class. The class discussed the rules, but now they need to write them down in their exercise books. This is their list but somebody has wiped away some words. Fill in the missing words.

Herr Jenkins und seine Klasse planen eine Lesenacht in der Schule. Er möchte deshalb mit der Klasse Regeln abmachen. Die Schüler haben die Regeln diskutiert und sie an die Tafel geschrieben. Nun sollen sie ins Heft abgeschrieben werden. Aber irgendjemand hat einige Wörter ausgewischt. Vervollständige die Regeln.

Rules for the night at school:

1. We ________________ bring any food because Mr Jenkins will bring some snacks with him.
2. We ________________ bring a blanket and a pillow because there are no beds at school!
3. We ________________ have a pen and some paper for questions!
4. We ________________ bring an MP3-Player because they are not allowed at school!
5. We ________________ bring our parents with us, Mr Jenkins will stay with us.
6. We ________________ tell anybody our story because it should be a surprise for everybody!
7. We ________________ bring any school books, this is a free time activity.
8. We ________________ laugh about others who are scared when they listen to the ghost stories!
9. We ________________ listen carefully to the other kids' stories because they could be on the next test!
10. We ________________ remember these rules because only then will the night be a success!

Lösungen

Welcome back

0.1 Focus on words: Holidays

a) Individuelle Lösungen.

b) Individuelle Lösungen.

c) 1 lake, 2 sea, 3 beach, 4 mountains, 5 Croatia, 6 France, 7 Spain, 8 Italy, 9 car, 10 plane, 11 train, 12 bus, 13 hotel, 14 caravan, 15 tent, 16 holiday flat, 17 swim, 18 take photos, 19 have fun, 20 ride a bike, 21 sunny, 22 warm, 23 rainy, 24 cloudy

Unit 1

1.1 Connecting the numbers

a) 1 describe, 2 dangerous, 3 amazing, 4 sights, 5 nothing, 6 explanation, 7 exciting, 8 argument, 9 unfriendly, 10 between, 11 flight, 12 fast, 13 after, 14 rude, 15 lend, 16 angry, 17 foreground

1.2 Describing pictures

a) In this picture you can see our **house**. It's the one on the right. My father's **car** is in front of our house. On the **left** there is another house, it's the Smith's house. Toby Smith and I like to play **football** in the afternoon. There is a field right next to our house. Many big **trees** grow along our street. There's also a **supermarket** next to Toby's house. You can buy nearly everything there. My sister and her friends are playing outside at the moment. They like to ride their **bikes** and play games.

b) In this picture **you can see a table**. It's time for **breakfast**! There are four people in my family, so there are four **plates** and four **cups**. In the middle of the table, there are two **bottles of orange juice** and tea. There is also some **butter** on a plate, some **marmalade** and **some bread**. Next to the bread is a big **bowl**. There are two **apples**, four **bananas** and some grapes in the bowl.

c) Individuelle Lösungen.

1.3 Role cards: Asking questions

Individuelle Lösungen.

1.4 Reading and writing: Tom's holidays in Croatia

b) 1 wrong, 2 right, 3 right, 4 wrong, 5 right, 6 wrong

1.5 Telling a story: Tom's first day at school

a) 3, 6, 7, 2, 8, 1, 5, 4

b) Individuelle Lösungen.

1.6 Information gap: The last party

Lösungen in der Tabelle des Partners.

Unit 2

2.1 Scrambled words

a) 1 outfit, 2 dress, 3 chips, 4 lemonade, 5 fashion, 6 sweets, 7 sandwich, 8 trainers, 9 pullover, 10 crisps, 11 milk, 12 trousers, 13 ice cream, 14 cola, 15 shorts, 16 chocolate, 17 baseball cap, 18 skirt, 19 orange juice, 20 boots

2.2 Information gap: Big, bigger, the biggest

Lösungen in der Tabelle des Partners.

2.3 Who's the youngest of the three?

Mögliche Lösungen:

a) Linda is as old as Toby, but Marc is younger than the two.
Linda is taller than Marc, but Toby is the tallest.
Toby has got more pets than Marc, but Linda has got the most pets.
Toby's family is bigger than Linda's, but Marc's family is the biggest.
Marc's hobby is more interesting than Toby's, but Linda's hobby is the most interesting.

b) Individuelle Lösungen.

2.4 Let's have a party!

a) We are going to have a **fancy dress party** on **Friday, 5th September** at **7pm** in **our classroom**. We are going to have a best costume competition, so dress up in your **most exciting costume**. Come and enjoy **great music and karaoke** …

b) Individuelle Lösungen.

2.5 What are you going to be?

b) Lösungswort: clown

2.6 At the party

Anna: Oh no. We haven't got **any** hot dogs left. Hurry up, Linda, we need **some** more. These hot dogs are the best in town. Everybody loves them.
Linda: OK, OK. I can go and make **some**. But are there enough orange juice and cola in the fridge, Marc?
Marc: Yes, everything is fine, ladies! This is going to be the best party in the world. Look! The people are having fun, they are dancing and laughing.

Anna: And most of the costumes are fantastic. **Some** children spent a lot of money on their costumes. But I think Peter and George's elephant costume is the best.
Marc: No, I don't think so. Tina's costume is much more exciting. She looks great in her short skirt and …
Linda: Oh, stop it, Marc! Have you seen Toby **anywhere**? He didn't look very happy in his costume.
Anna: He must be **somewhere**. I saw him a few minutes ago. He was talking to **some** girls in very nice sixties outfits. They liked his clown costume a lot.
Marc: Hmmm, there he is – on the dance floor with the girls. He looks happy now. Why isn't **anybody** dancing with me?
Linda: Poor Marc! Give me **something** to drink and help me with the hot dogs. Then we can go dancing.

Unit 3

3.1 Crossword: Animals

Lösungssatz: Be nice to animals.

3.2 When this lesson ends

Individuelle Lösungen.

3.3 What will you do if …?

Individuelle Lösungen.

3.4 Our crazy teacher

a) Mr. Funny is our **crazy** Music teacher. He always comes into our classroom in a **funny** way. He opens the door very **slowly**, and we only see his **big** and **round** head. Then he looks at us **strangely** and after that he comes in **quickly**. He sits down on his chair **carefully** and he closes his eyes **slowly**. Then he stands up again and starts to sing **terribly**. Mr. Funny can play the piano very **well**, but his voice is really **bad**. We have to listen to his favourite song in every lesson. He sings so **loudly** that sometimes the teacher from the class next to ours knocks at the door **angrily** and shouts: "Be **quiet**. Stop that **terrible** noise." But Mr. Funny thinks that he is a **wonderful** singer and he goes on and on and on …
At first, we had to laugh about this **strange** man, but now we think he is **crazy**.

b) Individuelle Lösungen.

3.5 TV – television

a) Mögliche Lösung:

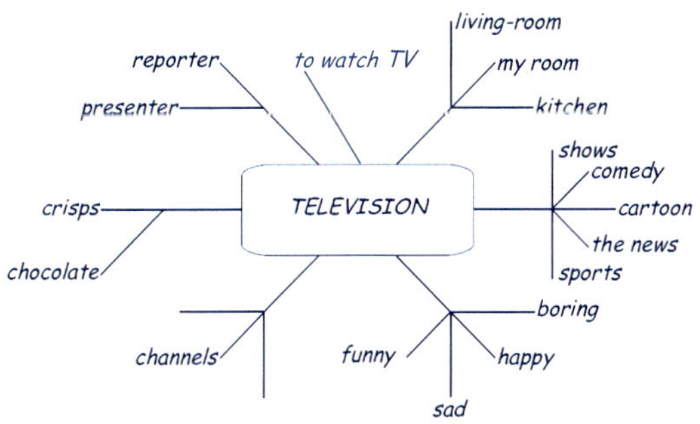

b) Individuelle Lösungen.

3.6 Do you know what these animals need?

a)

1 right
2 wrong – They don't sleep at night, they sleep during the day.
3 wrong – They aren't good at dancing, they are good at jumping.
4 right
5 wrong – They haven't got two legs, they have got four.
6 right
7 wrong – Milk is dangerous for them.
8 right
9 right
10 wrong – You should only touch them with gloves.

Unit 4

4.1 Parts of the body

a) Girl: finger, head, leg, mouth, shoulder, stomach, toe
Boy: arm, ear, eye, foot, hair, hand, knee, nose

b) Individuelle Lösungen.

c) headache, temperature, cold, sore throat, flu, toothache, broken leg, stomach ache

4.2 Word grid: Have you ever done this?

a)

m	d	c	o	o	k	e	d	n	p	a	q
e	e	i	o	l	m	j	u	e	d	d	b
t	k	l	s	w	h	v	n	t	b	e	k
d	a	r	p	u	m	d	k	t	a	h	r
d	r	o	p	p	e	d	l	i	y	c	t
o	s	s	r	b	n	u	o	r	f	t	n
p	h	a	d	a	o	i	p	w	z	a	o
p	a	b	a	s	d	k	k	l	u	w	l
t	f	o	e	v	o	o	p	b	d	j	l
u	t	t	r	a	v	e	l	l	e	d	m
w	s	e	f	h	u	b	s	l	v	t	b
a	o	w	p	s	d	g	k	l	o	a	o
c	l	z	n	a	w	r	q	o	m	b	t

b) cook, write, watch, drop, have, travel, lose, read, move

c), d), e) Individuelle Lösungen.

4.3 Word order

a)

1 Toby and Tina ride their bikes to school every morning.
2 We went to the zoo at the weekend.
3 I hate Maths tests a lot.
4 My father can play the trumpet.
5 They went on holiday to Spain this year.
6 You cannot win this game today.

b) Individuelle Lösungen.

4.4 An e-mail from Wales

a) Individuelle Lösungen.

b)

big smile	:)))
see you	cu
tomorrow	2morrow
sad, bad	:(
laughing out loud	lol
very big smile	:-D
surprise	o=
smile	:)

c), d), e) Individuelle Lösungen.

4.5 Can or may?

a)

1 I can count up to 100 in English.
2 Mum says, I may watch TV until 10 o'clock in the evening.
3 Our car cannot drive more than 120 km/h.
4 At schools today, our teachers may not hit us.

b)

1 … we weren't allowed to stay up late, the next day was a school day.
2 … our dog couldn't / wasn't able to go to the park, her leg was broken.
3 … our mum was very nice. She said we were allowed to sleep late.

c)

1 … our team will be able to win the game, because the other team is very bad.
2 … you will be able to see the sun again, because the clouds will be gone by then.
3 … he won't be able to swim with me in the pool, because today he hurt his foot.

d) **Tina:** Hi Simon. Nice to see you. **Can** you help me? I will have a party tomorrow.
Simon: Of course. **May/Can** I come, too?
Tina: Yes, but you **may** also bring a friend if you like.
Simon: Good. So how **can** I help you?
Tina: Tomorrow I **won't be allowed to** play loud music, so **can** you bring your guitar?
Simon: Yes, what else **can** I do?
Tina: Well, I **couldn't/wasn't able to** buy crisps yesterday, because the shops were closed, **can** you help me buy some now?
Simon: Yes, **can** I do something else for you?
Tina: I think that's all. But I **cannot** think clearly anymore, there are so many things to remember. I probably forgot something.
Simon: Don't worry, nobody **can** remember everything.

4.6 What happened?

Mögliche Lösungen:

a) **You:** Yes, I did.
You: The man on the bicycle was on Church Street. The woman in the car was on Abbey Road.
You: The woman in the car was not careful. She didn't stop at the stop sign. So the man crashed into the car. The man fell down on the street and hurt his leg. I think his leg is broken.

Unit 5

5.1 Town and country

a) post office, hotel, library, cinema, museum, theatre, supermarket, tourist information

b) Individuelle Lösungen.

c) hill, fields, farm, river, forest, valley, mountain, castle

d) Individuelle Lösungen.

5.2 Shopping in the city

Tina: Hey Toby, stop! I want to see this shop window. You are very tired, **aren't you**?
Toby: Of course I am. We have been walking around town for hours now. And you don't want to stop, **do you**?
Tina: No, I don't. I need a nice dress! How do you like this one? It's nice, **isn't it**?
Toby: Yes, it's alright. But what about the blue one you've got at home? It's still very modern, **isn't it**? You can wear it to the party, **can't you**?
Tina: No, I can't!!! I have already worn it at the last party. You don't mind if I try this one on, **do you**?
Toby: (suddenly looks excited!) No, I don't. There's a chair and some biscuits, great!
Tina: You won't eat too many, **will you**? We are going to have lunch with Jack and Ashley in 30 minutes.
Toby: Alright. But I can eat a lot, you know that, **don't you**? Hurry up and put on the dress, it could be the one, **couldn't it**?
Tina: You are making fun of me, **aren't you**? But you're right, I like it a lot, give me two minutes.
Toby: Tina? It's you, **isn't it**?
Tina: Yes, it's me, help please! I got stuck in the dress and I can't take it off!
Toby: Well, then we finally found your dress, **didn't we?** (he laughs)

5.3 Mind map: Your town

a), b) Individuelle Lösungen.

5.4 Irregular verbs

a) grow – grew, catch – caught, give – gave, steal – stole, know – knew, cut – cut, feel – felt, get – got, wear – wore, ride – rode, run – ran

b)

Solution: You are great!

5.5 A very hard week in the life of Jenny Brown

a)

1 Last Monday Jenny **had to make** posters for the concert.
2 On Tuesday at 3pm she **met** her band because they had to talk about their outfits for the concert.
3 They **had** a rehearsal at 6pm at the same say.
4 Two days later Jenny **talked to** a reporter from their school magazine. He wanted to do an interview with her.
5 After their very long rehearsal on Friday evening Jenny **argued** with her parents. They were angry because she came home so late that evening.
6 On Saturday night the concert **began** at 8 pm. When the concert was over she **was** very happy because everybody liked their show.

b)

1 Mike **has painted** a picture. Now he can put it on the wall.
2 His sister Helen **has finished** her homework. So she can listen to her new CD now.
3 Mike's mum **has done** the shopping for the weekend. So now she can read her exciting book.
4 John, Mike's friend, **has repaired** his bike. So now he can ride his bike to Mike's place.

c)

1 I can't come to your party tonight, because I **haven't finished** my homework yet.
2 My parents **got married** in 1990.
3 Last year we **went** on our holiday to Portugal.
4 Wow, that sounds great. I**'ve never been** there before.
5 **Have** you ever **read** an English book?
6 Yesterday we **went** on a trip to Berlin. That **was** very interesting.
7 I **started** to learn English two years ago.
8 Helen is so hungry. She **hasn't had** dinner yet.
9 I **have always wanted** to visit London. I **have heard** so many exciting stories about this city.
10 We **went** to the cinema last night and **watched** the new film with Brad Pitt.

5.6 Can you find the way to the rocket?

***will*-future**	***going to*-future**
X	X
X	X
X	X
X	X
X	X
X	X
X	X
X	X

Unit 6

6.1 Can you tell me the way, please?

a) Where's the hospital? *It's in Barton Street opposite the theatre.*
Where's the kindergarten? *It's in Green Park Road near the park and the river Avon.*
Where are the Roman Baths? *They're in York Street next to the Bath Abbey.*
Where's the cinema? *It's in Charlotte Street opposite the Queen Square.*

b), c) Individuelle Lösungen.

6.2 What's happening outside?

Mögliche Lösung:
There is a big road. People are driving their cars, some are riding their bikes. In the park behind the street, there are people who are running. Some are taking a walk or they are walking their dogs. There is a big empty space in the middle of the park, people are lying in the sun and some are reading books or the newspaper. Others are sleeping or using their phones. A family with two children is having a picnic. Three men are playing cards. In the background, there is a restaurant. People are having lunch or they are drinking a glass of water.

6.3 What were the students doing?

a) When Mrs Smith came into the classroom, Peter was drawing pictures on the board. Jane was standing on a chair. Jenny and Nick were talking to each other. Hanna was listening to music. Sue and Mel were reading magazines. Anne and Jeremy were eating sandwiches. Ron was doing his homework.

b) Individuelle Lösungen.

6.4 Who, which or that?

a)

1 What is the name of the first of the three ducks, **whose** uncle is Donald Duck?
2 Can you tell me the name of the animal, **which/that** lives in Australia?
3 I want to know the family name of the actor, **who/that** plays James Bond?
4 What is the family name of the author, **who/that** wrote the Harry Potter novels?
5 What is the name of the British capital, **which/that** starts with an L?

b)

	3▼					2▼	
		1►	T	I	C	K	
	C			5▼		A	
4►	R	O	W	L	I	N	G
	A			O		G	
	I			N		A	
	G			D		R	
				O		O	
				N		O	

c) In relative clauses you use who for people, use *which* for objects, can use that for people and objects, use *whose* for people but also for objects. In German, *whose* means 'dessen' or 'deren'. *Whose* is always followed by a noun.

6.5 Let's play a game!

Mögliche Lösungen:
plane: Your word describes a thing/something that can fly in the air.
doctor: Your word describes a person/somebody who works in a hospital.
elephant: Your word describes an animal that is very big and grey.
December: Your word describes the month that comes after November.
fireman: Your word describes a person/somebody who helps when there is a fire.
fish: Your word describes an animal that lives under water.
actor: Your word describes a person/somebody who plays roles in films.
shop assistant: Your word describes a person/somebody who works in a shop and sells things to you.
teacher: Your word describes a person/somebody who teaches subjects at school.
clock: Your word describes a thing/ something that tells you the time.
cat: Your word describes an animal that eats mice.
friend: Your word describes a person/somebody who meets you in the afternoon and plays with you.
dog: Your word describes an animal that can bark and be a very good friend to people.
pupil: Your word describes a person/somebody who goes to school to learn something there.
clown: Your word describes a person/somebody who is funny and has got a red nose.
budgie: Your word describes an animal that lives in a cage. It can be yellow, blue, green…
table: Your word describes a thing/something that you can find in a kitchen for example. You can put things on it.
board: Your word describes a thing/something that you can write on in your classroom. It's green.
cinema: Your word describes a place that shows films and sells popcorn.

6.6 A night at school

1 We **needn't** bring any food because Mr Jenkins will bring some snacks with him.
2 We **must** bring a blanket and a pillow because there are no beds at school!
3 We **must** have a pen and some paper for questions!
4 We **mustn't** bring an MP3-Player because they are not allowed at school!
5 We **needn't** bring our parents with us, Mr Jenkins will stay with us.
6 We **mustn't** tell anybody our story because it should be a surprise for everybody!
7 We **needn't** bring any school books, this is a free time activity.
8 We **mustn't** laugh about others who are scared when they listen to the ghost stories!
9 We **must** listen carefully to the other kids' stories because they can be part of the next class test!
10 We **must** remember the rules of the list because only then the night will be a success!